FLOWERS IN THE WINTER GARDEN

FLOWERS IN THE WINTER GARDEN

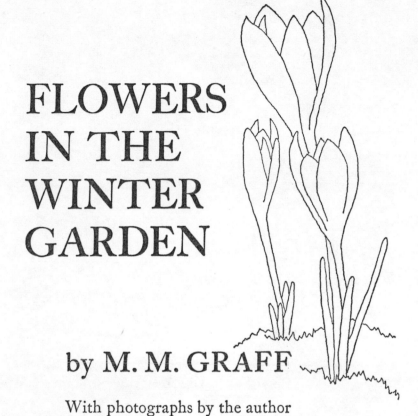

by **M. M. GRAFF**

With photographs by the author

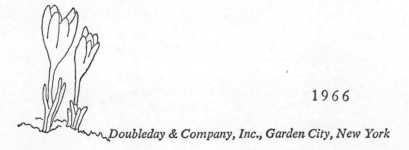

1966

Doubleday & Company, Inc., Garden City, New York

ACKNOWLEDGMENTS

Some of the photographs in this book and part of the text material in different form have appeared in *Flower & Garden, Horticulture, House & Garden, Popular Gardening,* and the New York *Times.* The author's thanks are extended to the editors of these publications for their courteous cooperation.

TABLE OF CONTENTS

ILLUSTRATIONS

INTRODUCTION

Every gardener with a dash of adventure and an ounce of skill can grow flowers outdoors in winter. All it takes is care in choosing a favorable spot, a list of suitable plants and bulbs, and a modest outlay for buying them.

Winter gardens are charged with excitement. When you plant your first bulb, you set the stage for a nerve-tingling melodrama: frail flowers pitted against a villainous climate. Even if you start as a spectator, I defy you to remain detached. The worse the weather gets, the more hotly you become involved with the fate of the flowers. Each predicted cold wave brings a new crisis of anxiety and outrage, which gives way to astonished relief when the flowers open unharmed through melting snow. I must add that the forces of winter win just often enough to keep an element of suspense in the outcome.

Besides filling the gray months with drama, winter gardens answer more particular needs. The plants themselves are small, requiring so little room that even the tiniest property can spare a corner for them. Several dozen bulbs will grow in a space the size of a man's handkerchief. The span of three bridge tables will accommodate bulbs by the hundreds, with carpeting plants to cover their sites during dormancy, and some accent plants for summer bloom.

Once the winter garden is built and planted, it needs little care—no spraying, staking, or pruning to command attention when beach or golf course are beckoning. Vacationers too can enjoy flowers in winter and set off for the summer without regret.

The winter-flowering plants and bulbs I will recommend have been tested in two gardens under widely varied circumstances. The first, in Manhasset, Long Island, was in rich, sandy loam on the south face of a hilltop; the second, in Tenafly, New Jersey, in heavy clay at the edge of wet woods. In the last year I have also studied plants in the Brooklyn Botanic Garden as they grow under city conditions.

All three gardens lie in Zone 7a (average minimum temperature 0° to 10° F.) yet growing conditions are by no means identical. Degrees of cold can be plotted on a chart, but not the subtler factors that affect plant hardiness. For example, the duration of freezing spells can be quite as critical as their severity. The complex influences that govern plant survival are outlined on the back of the Plant Hardiness Zone Map prepared by the U. S. Department of Agriculture and sold by the Superintendent of Documents, U. S. Government Printing Office, Washington, D.C. The map is handsomely printed in color and is large enough to show good detail. Altogether it is the best 15¢ investment a gardener can make. With its help you can work out a reasonably good guess as to how a plant will perform in your particular section of the country.

The population of the winter garden varies with the climate. Broadly speaking, bulbs have the widest range of tolerance. They duck underground after flowering and, in dry areas, benefit by the baking of our near-tropical summers. The proportion of woody plants increases as you move southward: shrubs and trees that fail in Zone 7a will get by in Philadelphia and are standard garden subjects in Virginia. Alpine plants, on the other hand, require a long winter's rest, preferably under an unbroken snow cover. These do their best in the cool areas of New England, southern Canada, and the Pacific Northwest. Since many alpines and species bulbs form their buds while still under the snow, theirs will be the first flowers of spring.

Since the observations in this book are drawn from firsthand experience in testing and evaluating plants in my gardens, the judgments I reach are necessarily colored by personal preferences. Knowing that one man's crimson may be another's magenta, I have tried to give the reasons behind my verdicts of praise or disdain.

In general I have followed the Royal Horticultural Society's *Dictionary of Gardening*. Published in 1956 with a supplement, the second edition is up to date on changes and corrections made in recent years. Color designations are based on the RHS Horticultural Colour Chart.

Since this is a book for gardeners and not a scientific treatise, I have sometimes sacrificed botanical precision to simplicity. For one thing I use the word "bulb" rather loosely. It seems pedantic and needlessly distracting to insist on distinguishing between bulb, corm, tuber, and rhizome. For the gardener's purpose they can be lumped together since they are handled in much the same way.

Scientific descriptions of plants deal with measurable data: height, color, shape of leaf, number of stamens, and the like. My response to flowers is too impassioned for mere statistics. Enthusiasm sometimes leads me to speak of favorites as if they had personality or even purpose. Since this implies consciousness, it is guaranteed to bring any proper botanist to an instant rolling boil. Nevertheless the intrinsic charm of a flower lies in its emotional impact. To say that it is demure, jaunty, bold, or reticent conveys its quality far more vividly than to state its height in inches. I believe I can communicate my joy in the living plant better in human terms than in scientific ones, even at the price of compounding a fallacy.

I can't tell for certain when I first tasted the delights of winter gardening. In the lightheaded abandon of moving, I threw away my earliest garden records. I can however place my first trial between brackets: after 1942 when we bought the Manhasset house, and before 1946 when the noted plantsman William Craig retired.

My first winter-flowering bulbs came from Mr. Craig. Though chiefly famed for his lilies, he is remembered most warmly—on my part at least—for his introduction of uncommon bulbs. It was these little-known wildings that burst the bounds of my garden horizon, opening endless fields for exploration and adventure.

I wrote Mr. Craig on his retirement to tell him how much pleasure his bulbs had brought me. I must have sensed the promise of this new aspect of gardening even though I had barely crossed the threshold of experimenting with winter flowers. Since then, my debt of gratitude to William Craig has grown with the years. I wish I could thank him now from a full heart.

I can however express my liveliest gratitude and affection to Nelva M. Weber, L.A., for sharing her knowledge of plants and how to group them effectively; to Carl Starker, valued equally as supplier of rare plants and of directions for planting them; and to Ralph Bailey and John Everett for encouragement and guidance in preparing this book. I am also indebted to the staff of the Brooklyn Botanic Garden, most particularly the Director, Dr. George S. Avery, Jr.; Robert S. Tomson, Assistant Director; and Charles McGinley who opened the rock garden for my study. My warmest thanks go also to George Kalmbacher, Taxonomist, for his invaluable technical assistance; and to Marie G. Giasi, Librarian, who spared no effort to make my research easy and fruitful.

I am indebted to all these friends and many others who have helped me to fill four seasons with beauty and interest. Perhaps the best way to express my gratitude is to share my experiments with inquiring gardeners—enough to indicate a starting point but not so fully that you miss discovering for yourselves the fun of winter gardening.

1

Starting from Scratch

When you plan a winter garden, concentrate on January. During autumn and early winter, flowers proceed on schedule with no help on your part. It's after Christmas when the ground is solidly frozen that the canny gardener's bag of tricks begins to pay off. If you have created a favorable microclimate, plants that ordinarily flower in March in the open garden will bloom for you in January.

Each winter garden must be tailored to measure. Since every house and plot is unique in orientation, terrain, air flow, and water movement, no single blueprint can be stretched to fit. Instead, the gardener must know something of the normal cycle of the plants he will use, and how to modify this cycle to promote the earliest possible bloom.

At first gasp the prospect of flowers surviving the extremes of a northern winter seems impossible. And so it is, if you are thinking in terms of man-made garden hybrids, as unfit for roughing it in the open as cage-bred canaries.

Winter gardens call for tough plants, resilient enough to adapt to wide swings in temperature, and so rugged that their flowers are uninjured at 10° F. or below. Alpines are the obvious choice. As natives of high altitudes, they are hardened by bitter cold and by short but hot summers, conditions even more grueling than they are likely to meet in cultivation.

There's a saying that high mountains have two seasons: winter and August. This means that alpine plants must bloom, ripen seed, and store food between the melting of snowbanks in late July and the new snows of September. Not an hour of this short summer can be wasted in preparation. While snow is still several feet deep, growth begins under its translucent roof. By the time the snowbank recedes, the plants are fully formed and budded—pale, crumpled, muddy, but ready to spring erect and open their flowers almost as you watch.

In our less orderly climate where winter temperatures zigzag across the freezing mark, alpine bulbs still obey their mountain timetable. Sometimes in a fit of impatience I've shoveled a deep snowdrift from my garden and found crocus buds pushing out of their sheaths, tightly furled but ready to fly open at a touch of sun. When the ground is deeply frozen in snowless winters, bulbs inch up more slowly, gaining ground with each brief noonday thaw until a mild day brings their flowers bubbling from the earth.

As you see, alpine plants come to you already primed for a racing start, needing only a few thaws to spark them into bloom. If you arrange for early thawing, you can enjoy spring in January.

CHOOSING THE SPOT

The first step is to select a naturally warm site. As you study your property you will notice areas where snow drifts deeply and stays long, and others where it starts to melt as soon as the sun shines. Obviously the latter is the choice for a winter garden.

Usually the ideal exposure is at the base of a wall facing south, where the sun's heat is intensified by reflection. It is difficult to believe the potency of such a solar oven unless you have experienced it. One bright February noon as I took pictures at the south wall, quite comfortable in a light sweater with the sleeves pushed up, a neighbor rushed out to warn me of certain pneumonia. To reassure her I fetched a thermometer: it read 30° in the open and 71° on the ground beside the plants.

The evidence of rapid melting tells you where to locate your winter garden. To this basically favored microclimate, you can add other factors to trap and retain heat. No matter if each makes a difference of only a few degrees. The total may nudge the thermometer well above the freezing point.

To the south wall, add a south slope to exert a three-way influence on the temperature. Since the winter sun is low in the sky, its rays glance off flat areas but are intercepted and absorbed by a slope. For a second benefit, consider that cold air is heavy: it flows harmlessly from high places and gathers in frost pools on level ground and in hollows. Lastly, dry soils warm faster than wet, so a sharply drained incline may thaw when heavy soil at its foot is still locked in ice. Add some deeply sunken rocks to soak up heat by day and release it slowly during the night, and you have a clear picture of the form a winter garden should take.

A south-facing rock garden with a wall at its back incorporates most of the factors that lead to early bloom. Happily, cultural and aesthetic needs go hand in hand. A rock garden, a mountainside in miniature, approximates the natural habitat of alpine plants and gives them a visual setting as well. Since the plants are small, they would be lost in an open border. They need to be grouped closely in an intimate garden scaled to their size, just as diamonds are displayed in a small shadowbox to concentrate attention on the jewels and to minimize the actual expanse of the show window.

If other circumstances permit, the winter garden should be located below the most used windows of the house to lift your spirits every time you pass by. Since the main living areas of a house are usually turned to the sun, this is apt to be the south side, though not invariably by any means. The wings of a courtyard or the sheltered angle between two walls may exert a double influence, trapping the sun's heat and blocking the cold wind that dissipates it.

Such an alternate site should be chosen if the south wall is overhung with shade trees. The winter garden has reached peak bloom long before trees come into leaf so flowering is not directly affected. However, many bulbs require a summer baking and may not ripen under dense shade. Also, drip from branches is damaging to delicate plants, digging channels in creepers and battering small treasures like cyclamen and androsaces to death. Trees at some distance are an advantage, as their moving shadow tempers the full blast of noonday heat without cutting off sky light, and leaves the bed open to morning and afternoon sun.

By watching for the first patches of bare earth after snow, you will find odd corners that invite a handful of bulbs: the base of a chimney, perhaps, or an areaway warmed by cellar windows. When you order more bulbs than your garden will hold (as I always do) or when your stock needs dividing, it's nice to put the overflow in out-of-the-way places such as these, where you can cut nosegays for the house without robbing the main display. Make a note also to put a few bulbs by a porch or entry where they can be admired at close range without putting on galoshes, and don't forget a patch of crocuses by the back door so that you can bring in a note of cheer along with the milk.

Besides looking for spots that thaw quickly, take a cue from the behavior of established bulbs. For several years I had unaccountably early bloom along a wall that faced somewhat north of east. Since this was a wretched exposure to start with, and out of the public eye, I used the space to grow daffodils for cutting. Daffodils at the base of the wall were in full flower while their companions at the edge of the bed, four feet away, were barely above ground. I could only guess that some freak of reflection from a neighbor's white house must have warmed that otherwise shaded strip. A northeast aspect wouldn't be my choice but on the assumption that bulbs know what they like better than I do, I put a few crocuses close to the wall. Even though newly planted, they opened eight days before those in what I had considered an ideal spot, a snug corner facing south and east.

Broadly, then, put your winter garden where thaws naturally come early, and use every possible stratagem to intensify the sun's heat and reduce the chilling effect of wind. If I can't point precisely to the best spot on your property, I trust I have supplied a thermal divining rod so that you can find it for yourself.

BUILDING THE WINTER GARDEN

Once you have chosen the location you can start collecting rocks. Anyone who has a natural outcrop or a block and tackle to build a convincing replica can skip this part. For most of us, material for the do-it-yourself rockery is limited to what two people can heave into a station wagon or car trunk. This is admittedly a handicap, as only massive rocks can give a feeling of true stability. In order to minimize the spotty effect of small rocks, it is essential to keep strictly to one color and type. A common mistake is to combine weathered boulders, freshly blasted rock, pink granite, pepper-and-salt aggregate, and stone glinting with mica. Instead of suggesting a natural rock formation, the result is a dump. If you collect rocks of one color only, you can piece them, grouping three or four to look like one large slab, or simulating a ledge by lining out several in one plane. Sempervivums and creepers such as I will describe in the last chapters make excellent camouflage for such patchwork, chinking the cracks or draping them so that the joints are invisible.

The ideal material for building a garden is sedimentary rock. As this was deposited in layers, it breaks into slabs or chunks with relatively flat top and bottom. Pound for pound, a flat rock presents more usable surface than a rounded one, since no weight is wasted on hidden bulges. In addition, cliffs and ledges built of flat rock are stable, not dangerously wobbly or subject to heaving by frost. The joints are tight, exposing very little soil to the washing action of rain. The deep crevices they form make perfect settings for choice alpine plants.

Beautifully grained ledge rock, ornamented with moss and lichen, is a joy to use. With its look of age, it gives the newest rockery an established air. The only care needed is to keep the lines of stratification parallel. Whether horizontal or tilted, entire or broken by faults, the strata should all thrust at the same angle.

If you haven't access to a supply of ledge rock, you must make do with what is available. In New Jersey I used the local red sandstone because there was more of that on the property than of other sorts. Porous stone of this kind benefits plants by storing moisture and also grows a becoming coat of moss. The shapes were uninteresting, as soft stone wears smooth, but the warm color was quite pleasing in contrast with foliage greens.

The color of sandstone created a difficulty which I hadn't foreseen. The crushed stone sold for driveway surfacing is light blue or grayish, impossible to blend with a red-brown background. When I wanted stone chips I had to make them myself, hammering chunks of sandstone on the driveway like a convict at a rock pile.

Soft stones with rounded surfaces can't be piled one on another to form cliffs. If this rules out a mountainside, you can still reproduce the gentler slopes at its base. In these the underlying rock is mantled by gritty debris from the cliffs above, and shows only as a vertical face where the ground drops to another level. In building these terraced meadows, keep the outline irregular, swelling in and out in promontories and bays.

If you can forget the straight edge, an alpine meadow is built much like a staircase. Choose the biggest rocks you can handle for the risers, that is, the exposed face of the outcrop. Where edges don't abut tightly, wedge smaller stones behind the joint and pack any remaining holes with gravel.

Since we are dealing with odd-shaped rocks, not rectangular but possibly tapering or rounding off toward the top, a row of them may look like ladyfingers around a charlotte russe. To restore the illusion of a ledge, finish the upper surface with flat-topped stones. These should be fitted as closely as possible into the hollows between the risers, and placed so that their far sides disappear under the soil of the meadow. If the piecing is carefully done—and you will understand now why I stressed the importance of keeping to rocks of one color— the completed job should pass for a solid outcrop. Any defects can be hidden behind a drapery of creeping plants.

For optimum steadiness, each succeeding tier should probably rest on a hidden rock foundation. I say "probably" because I don't do it myself: I've never had enough rocks to squander where they don't show, and besides I'm incapable of precise planning in advance. In a way, I don't want to be held to a set plan. Half the fun of building a garden is making it up as you go along. I like to improvise, trying various groupings, shifting rocks until they look right, and letting the character of the garden evolve from the material that forms it. In other words, I can't tell where the second tier is going to begin until the first is complete and the plateau behind it filled with prepared soil. Then I start building the next setback, taking care to sink each rock deeply enough so that it won't teeter when I step on it. Admittedly this is a slapdash style of construction, perhaps possible only because I don't weigh a great deal. More conscientious and foresighted craftsmen, and heavier ones, will very likely build a stone foundation to support each tier of rock.

The gradual incline of an alpine meadow is less dramatic than a cliff garden and affords fewer crevices for high alpine plants. On the credit side, its plateaus accommodate broad colonies of bulbs. Since these are the mainstay of the winter garden, a sweep of alpine meadow will be more flowery than an austere rock face.

Of all forms of rock, the most difficult to work with are boulders such as I had in Manhasset. When the glacier emptied its pockets to form Long Island, it deposited a small boy's collection of varicolored rocks, most of them round as bowling balls and nearly as impermeable. On trips to Westchester and Connecticut, we loaded the trunk with shapely rock until the tailpipe struck sparks at every bump. Even so it was necessary to use boulders for the basic construction and save the ledge rock for facing.

The trouble with boulders, mechanically speaking, is that they abut at only one point on their circumference. Obviously it isn't possible to make a tight joint. If rain water isn't slowed, it will sluice between the boulders and behind their point of contact, cutting gullies that expose roots at the top of the slope and bury plants at its bottom. If you are compelled to support a bank with boulders, be sure to reinforce the soil between them with tough, thickset shrubs or densely matted creepers. Plants suitable for the job will be found in Chapter 9.

The best way to deal with boulders is to stop fighting them. No amount of wrestling will convert glacial litter into honest, bone-of-the-earth rock strata. Instead, accept their limitations and place them where they would occur in nature. Set deeply into a slope, a well-matched group will pass for the outliers of a buried outcrop, scoured smooth by the action of a passing glacier. A similar group rising slightly above a gravel plain could be the remains of a sunken ledge.

Boulders survived glaciation because of extreme hardness. Their density admits no water, as lack of moss indicates. As a result they are of no benefit to plants and may indeed be harmful if set high on the ground. With most of their surface exposed to the sun, they absorb and radiate heat with such intensity that nearby plants are injured. A deeply sunk boul-

der, though it stores no water, can at least offer a cool retreat
for deep-rooted plants.

For cultural and aesthetic reasons, *never* try to make boulders look bigger by standing them on their thin edge or—worse
yet—on one end like an egg in a cup. It may seem a waste of
material, but it is absolutely essential to sink boulders below
their greatest diameter. When they sit so high that you can
see the in-curve below their waistline, they are revealed as
contemptible stones. If they are still growing as they enter the
soil, their size is as limitless as your imagination.

Since boulders can't be fitted tightly together, the gaps between them must be masked with a strong-growing plant. Prostrate junipers are perfect in scale and rugged appearance and
will tolerate a hot, cramped situation. *Juniperus squamata
prostrata* is only a few inches high but is capable of covering
an area of three or four square feet. Its growth is dense and
compact, and of a soft fresh green with a silver-blue cast. It
billows over rocks in a charming way, hugging their contours
and effectively masking joints. *J. horizontalis* 'Bar Harbor' is
deservedly famous for its frosty blue coloring but may be too
rapid a grower for a small garden. *J. h.* 'Blue Horizon' is sea
green with elongated gray tips, quite prostrate but making a
wavy pattern that is especially beautiful as a cascade over a
rock face. Cotoneasters such as *C. horizontalis* can be pegged
down to cover a group of boulders, but as they are not evergreen in the North, they make a screen for summer only.

A sloping plain of boulders, coarse gravel, and stone chips
is often called a moraine from its resemblance to the rubble
at the sides and toe of a glacier. In a lowland garden, however,
there is no animating stream of icy water running under the
surface, so the term "scree" is more accurate. By any name,
the boulder garden is hot and dry, a perfect situation for bulbs
that want a summer baking and for mat-forming plants like
dianthus and armeria that abhor dampness. High alpine
plants that need a cool root run have a hard time in scree,

but may find refuge in a pocket of humus under the north side of a half-buried rock.

To sum up, the less desirable the rock, the more work is needed to arrange it satisfactorily. In the end, the handy boulders on your property may cost more time and backache than hunting out a supply of ledge rock.

PREPARING THE SOIL

In order to prepare soil in the right proportions, it is well to make a master plan that divides the garden into acid and alkaline sections. As a general rule, plants that want acid soil also like moisture and some shade. If your garden is in an L with one wall facing west, or if a portion is shaded by trees at a distance, this is the best aspect for primroses, ferns, hellebores, *Eranthis hyemalis*, and anemones. Soil for this section should be rich in humus—peat, leafmold, aged manure—with enough coarse sand to keep it friable.

Turning now to the sunny area, continue the acid soil a little way for ericas, callunas, gentians, *Phlox subulata*, and a few other nonconformists. The soil should again be well supplied with humus but with a greater measure of sand for free aeration.

A neutral zone follows the sun-acid section. It is composed of good garden loam with some sand and humus added, and bonemeal for its alkaline reaction. If the basic soil is strongly acid, ground limestone should be mixed in to offset the excess. This stretch is for the amiable middle-of-the-road plants that make no emphatic demands but get along happily in ordinary soil. When plants are described without any note of soil preference, they belong to this agreeable company.

Beyond the buffer zone of neutral soil comes the limestone section. Winter bloom isn't at stake here, for most species bulbs are indifferent to lime or its absence. (Lime-loving cyclamen and bulbous irises are exceptions.) The purpose of the alkaline section is to keep the winter garden colorful throughout the year. Many of the most charming and long-flowering creepers and accent plants of the early spring and summer prefer lime soil: aubrieta, armerias, campanulas, and dianthus head a long list.

If a winter garden is your sole interest, let me stress that you can ignore elaborate rock structures. All the plants you want will grow and flourish on a simple terraced slope. Those who want a winter garden with the least possible effort are advised to skip directions for building cliffs and crevices.

CREVICE BUILDING AND PLANTING

The challenge of difficult alpines is a specialized field, one that appeals more to experienced gardeners than to beginners. When easy plants lose their capacity to surprise, there's new excitement in trying impossible ones. In the limestone section of the winter garden, cherished alpine jewels have a fighting chance.

Unlike bulbs which require a summer baking, high alpine plants must never parch at the root. In nature they grow in blazing sun on a dry rock face, insulated against any possible dampness by a cushion of gritty debris, yet with their roots constantly bathed by icy water from snowfields above.

Of course it's impossible to duplicate alpine conditions in the lowlands, but plants are surprisingly adaptable if you approximate their needs. The trick is to confine and direct their roots, compelling them to reach deep into the cool recesses of the slope. This is done by building a crevice, in effect a sandwich of flattish rocks with the roots of the plants in gritty soil for the filling.

In placing crevice rocks, be sure that they slant downward from front to back. In this position, water quickly drains away from sensitive crowns and is conducted to the roots. In the bank behind the rocks put a lifetime supply of humus lightened with sand and mixed with ground limestone, bonemeal, and dry manure to make a reservoir of moisture and nutriment.

Rosetted plants such as sempervivums and androsaces can be poked into the slit of an existing crevice with a good chance of survival. More complex root systems—those of shrubs and woody creepers, and fleshy taproots like those of campanulas and armerias—should be set in place while the crevice is being built. This is the only sure way to extend roots to their fullest and to make certain that no air spaces remain between the sandwiching rocks.

When the bottom rock is settled, place small stone wedges at intervals for the upper stone to rest on, and spread gritty soil over the surface. Put a handful of gravel under the crown of the plant, coax its roots back as far as they will go, and pack the whole sandwich tightly with more gritty soil before setting on the top slice. Test this rock for steadiness, and add more wedges if necessary until it will hold your weight without sliding or rocking. Be sure to pack the rich prepared soil firmly against the back edges of the rocks and between them. The root channel must be continuous, joining the bank without any air space, or your labor and plant will be lost.

Of course the rocks forming a crevice aren't isolated, but lined out side by side to form a continuous ledge. Other layers can be added above the first, set back in a series of steps or forming a steep cliff as you prefer. If your project is an ambitious one, you can add realism and variety by breaking the strata to imitate natural faulting, or by creating a deep ravine to frame an imaginary waterfall.

As I've said, these directions are for dedicated alpinists. Let's tune in the casual gardener again. Crevices may be ideal but there are easier ways to modify lowland hardships, though to a limited degree of effectiveness. The gritty plateaus of an alpine meadow, sharply drained and sloped to catch the sun, are perfect for winter bulbs both in bloom and at rest. The plants that cover their sites may suffer during our long, hot summers. A mulch of stone chips serves to deflect the rays of the sun, thus reducing soil temperature and loss of water by evaporation. For especially sensitive plants, you can excavate the north side of a deeply sunken rock and stuff the cavity with humus to make a cool root haven.

A GARDEN-VIEWING WALK

Regardless of its type, a rock garden is a re-creation of mountain scenery. The illusion of wildness would be shattered by a neat lawn at its foot. (Appearance aside, the job of clipping grass against rough rocks is a tedious and knuckle-skinning one.) A broad walk of flagstones laid in sand makes a good buffer between rocks and lawn. An aluminum barrier should of course be sunk on the lawn side to keep grass in its place.

A sand-laid walk dries quickly, especially if it is built with a slight pitch to one side. A drop of two inches to ten feet isn't noticeable but is enough to keep puddles from standing. After rain or snow, the garden can be viewed in comfort from a flagged path long before grass is dry enough to walk on. Moss should be encouraged to dress cracks between the stones, and a few plants of creeping thyme make a filmy decoration.

Stingy walks are one of the commonest errors in garden design. Instead of saving space, they diminish the apparent size of the property. Make your garden-viewing path at least six feet wide so that visitors can walk abreast without sidling. With room to spare, the creepers that drape the lowest tier of rocks can spill over the paving at their base. Free-growing plants give continuity to the design, linking rockery and walk and blurring the transition between them.

Put away the crowbar: the hard work is done. It's time to turn to catalogues for the reward of your labor.

ORDERING AND PLANTING BULBS

Species bulbs have a very short shelf life, unlike gladioli and garden daffodils which general dealers handle like canned goods. For this reason it is important to order from bulb specialists who thoroughly understand how to pack and when to ship highly perishable material. *Hyacinthus azureus, Leucojum vernum, Sternbergia lutea,* cyclamen, and bulbous irises grow mushy and mildewed if kept out of the ground too long. Anemones and eranthis, rhizomatus plants which are classed as bulbs for convenience, are intolerant of moving except in full growth. In storage they quickly dry out and become in fact the dead sticks they resemble. Fall-blooming bulbs like colchicums and autumnal crocuses must be ordered in midsummer for early delivery, and planted on arrival so that they can make some root growth before they flower. If you get these tricky bulbs from an inexperienced dealer or from a bin in the hardware store, you are paying a high price for humus.

Except for miniature narcissus and cyclamen, most of the species bulbs are quite flexible about planting depth. The rule of thumb is to set a bulb so that it will be covered with earth two or three times its height. In other words, a 1″ bulb goes into a 3″ hole with 2″ of soil above its tip. My own preference is for rather deep planting, with the aim of putting the bulbs below the digging range of squirrels and chipmunks. This may possibly delay their flowering but I'd rather have late bloom than a hole in the ground. In any case, many of the bulbs can adjust their depth to suit their requirements. Crocuses can change their level by means of a slanting starch root which develops a new corm at its tip. Chionodoxas, by producing new bulbs at the base of the old, will work themselves down below the reach of a trowel so that an established clump must be lifted with a spade.

Touchy bulbs like irises should be completely encased in sand so that they are insulated from fungus-bearing humus particles. When planting a wide drift of crocuses, I usually allow for a layer of sand below, around, and over them, reasoning that a loose stratum should favor free increase. Sand acts as a safeguard also: if you dig carelessly without consulting your chart, yellow sand will flash a warning at the first turn of a trowel.

KEEPING RECORDS

A chart is a permanent record of identification, far better than stakes or labels that get lost or defaced and in any case violate the naturalness of a garden. A label gives only the name of a planting and not its boundaries, though the latter information is vital when working along dormant bulbs.

Twenty-inch shelf paper makes good chart material, being durable and long enough to need no piecing. If each end is taped to a paper core and rolled around it, any section can be examined without leaving loose ends to flap in the wind and get torn or dirty. I used a scale of $2'' = 1'$, first ruling off two-inch squares and then sketching (later inking) the ground plan of terraces and rocks. With these as landmarks, it is easy to record plants and bulbs as you put them in. Before covering a group of bulbs, be sure to draw the outline of the space each variety occupies, and note in it the name, the number planted, the supplier's name, and the date. If the chart is faithfully kept, bulbs can be added in future years without overplanting, and ground covers can be moved or divided without slicing the bulbs that lie beneath.

MAINTENANCE

Once planted, the maintenance of a winter garden consists of good housekeeping. The watchful gardener needs no printed schedule. It becomes automatic to perform little attentions on every trip past the garden: to pluck out infant weeds while their roots are still feeble; to pick out leaves that blow in and lodge among dwarf shrubs; and to remove yellow foliage before it attracts slugs.

An exception to the last is bulb foliage, which must be allowed to ripen fully. As Philip Miller cautioned in his masterly *Gardener's Dictionary* of 1807: "The green leaves . . . should not be cut off until they decay, notwithstanding they appear a little unsightly; for by cutting off the leaves, the roots will be so weakened as not to arrive at half their usual bigness, nor will their flowers the succeeding year be half so large." Miller's wisdom is proved by the failure of crocuses "naturalized" in lawns according to a durable misconception. Shorn of their leaves, they die as surely as daffodils cut to the ground after flowering by the gangs of handymen (self-termed gardeners) who ravage suburban properties in their care.

Spent flowers and their stalks are in general best tidied away. Free seeders like *Hyacinthus azureus* and the muscaris should be beheaded as soon as the flowers fade. Conversely, choice plants that increase slowly except by seed should be closely watched and their capsules gathered as soon as ripe. If left to open naturally, the whole crop may be carried off by ants. A close clipping after bloom keeps dwarf shrubs—ericas, iberis—neat and compact, and prevents carpeting plants from growing stringy and threadbare.

The winter garden needs very little fertilizing. Its plants are self-sufficient wildings, not inflated hybrids that need chemical transfusions to sustain them. An annual fall dressing of screened compost and sand is beneficial. It replaces any soil washed away in heavy rains and helps to anchor the season's new rosettes and runners. I also scatter some bonemeal over the bulb plantings, though I think this may be more an expression of benevolence than any real need.

PESTS AND DISEASES

Species bulbs and alpines are remarkably free of the thrips, mites, viruses, and blights that afflict artificially reared garden giants. Plants from high altitudes are preselected by nature. In the struggle for survival, frail and disease-prone varieties are weeded out and only the toughest plants persist.

Failure with wildings can usually be traced to faulty handling either in transit or in planting. Soft rot and molds result from baking in the hold of a ship, delay at Quarantine, bruising in the mail, and long storage by dealers ignorant of the need for early shipment. Dank, poorly aerated soil is a major cause of loss from basal rot, mildew, crown rot, and other fungus infections. The best prevention of disease is to reproduce the plants' alpine habitat: lean, gritty soil on a slope that faces the sun.

I wish that pests could be dealt with as briskly as diseases. By its very nature, the winter garden is plagued with vermin. A feast of succulent greenery in midwinter must inevitably attract starving rabbits, while chipmunks, mice, and squirrels devour bulbs at all seasons.

CHIPMUNKS, according to bitter complaints, can be as destructive to bulb plantings as squirrels are. My garden was spared this damage, possibly because adjoining oak woods supplied acorns without the need of digging.

My quarrel with chipmunks is based not on their greed but on their subway systems. When chipmunks burrow under a rock, no predator can dig them out. Rock gardens are therefore favored homesites: the colony increases unchecked, and with it the expanding network of tunnels and caverns. The extent of the mining operations may not be suspected until rocks begin to sink and plants die with their roots in an air pocket.

Control of burrowing animals with Cyanogas is effective but dangerous, and is mentioned with the sternest cautions. Unlike poisons which may be eaten by birds, the effect of the gas is restricted to its target—and bird lovers must weigh this advantage against the very real risk to themselves. In preparation, cover all but one entrance hole with tar paper, tarpaulin, or plastic held down with bricks. After sunset when the chipmunks are underground, take a deep breath and hold it, shake some Cyanogas into the open hole, cover it quickly, and run for fresh air.

I don't know whether the rat killer Warfarin will work on other rodents but it may be worth trying. It is supposedly not injurious to birds but I would play safe by using a funnel or long-handled spoon to place the meal as deeply as possible into the burrow.

CUTWORMS feed at night and hide in the ground by day. Their presence is advertised by the bleeding stubs of tender stems and leaves which they cut off an inch or less above soil level. Cutworms very often bury themselves near the base of a juicy victim so that they can finish it off the following night. The fat, dark gray caterpillars usually stay just below the surface and can readily be scratched up and squashed. If the villain can't be located without damaging the roots of the plant, dust some DDT or chlordane around the base and water it in.

MICE and MOLES working together can decimate a bulb planting. Moles are blamed for eating bulbs on the evidence of their telltale runs. As a fact, they tunnel in search of root-eating grubs and might be considered beneficial to gardens if their energetic burrowing didn't heave bulbs and plants out of the ground and—far worse—provide runways for mice. It is the mice, working unseen, that actually eat the bulbs.

Control is a two-pronged attack. For immediate results, put Warfarin in the burrows to dispose of mice. Cyanogas is of doubtful effect since burrows usually crack open at the top and would not contain the gas. For long-range protection, grub-proof the entire property with chlordane or its equivalent. If moles have to go elsewhere for food, mice will no longer be able to use their tunnels to get at bulbs.

RABBITS are the worst ravagers of the winter garden, especially when snow covers their normal browse. None of the old wives' remedies—moth balls, empty bottles, or dried blood—will turn a hungry rabbit from a patch of crocuses in delectable leaf and flower. Shooting is the most effective curb, taking care to aim from an upper porch or window so that the bullet goes into the ground. If the neighborhood is too closely built up to permit shooting safely, then a two-foot chicken-wire fence is the only infallible protection.

The bark of young dogwoods, flowering cherries, and the like is a favorite rabbit delicacy. Trunks should be wrapped for two feet above the probable snow level with several thicknesses of aluminum foil, securely tied so that no winter gale can work it loose. Multiple-stemmed shrubs such as azaleas, corylopsis, fothergilla, and flowering quince—all rabbit manna—are difficult to enclose, as are climbing roses trained on a low rail fence. Among my roses was the *rugosa* hybrid 'Dr. Eckener,' too ferociously spiny to gather barehanded, yet one winter gnawed clean of thorns, bark, and cambium from the snow line to the height of a rabbit on tiptoe. In succeeding years all vulnerable shrubs were sprayed with a heavy coat of arsenate of lead, using Wiltpruf as a fixative. Arsenic must act as a repellent as well as a permanent cure. If any sprayed shrubs were nibbled, the damage was too slight to be noticed.

Lead arsenate is colored candy pink, an inappropriate choice for a stomach poison. The residue can be tolerated on the canes of roses and other deciduous shrubs as it is quickly concealed when spring growth gets under way. I don't use it on evergreen shrubs, however, as the stain is persistent. Traces of it may still discolor the foliage at flowering time. For this reason I prefer to protect dwarf azaleas by caging them in chicken wire, closing it over the top in case snowdrifts give rabbits a leg up.

SLUGS are gluttons for tender growth. With their rasplike mouth parts, they can wipe out seedlings, destroy soft stems, and skeletonize new leaves and buds. The cause of damage is not always recognized, as slugs are easy to overlook. They feed by night, hide by day, and roll into inconspicuous pebble-colored balls if disturbed. The slimy trails they leave are conclusive evidence.

Slugs like to hide under damp surfaces. Even if all wet, rotting leaves are scrupulously cleaned away, ferns and mat-forming plants still afford shelter. To protect the foliage and flowers of small bulbs, campanulas, and primroses—all favored by slugs—it is necessary to use poison.

I used Metameal, a metaldehyde-bran preparation put out by Garfield Williamson, Jersey City, New Jersey. This is dry and pleasant to handle, ready to use from the bag with no mixing or spraying. It is placed around vulnerable plants in little mounds, a tablespoon or so in each spot, and should be renewed when no dying slugs are found nearby. The effect of Metameal is dramatic and highly gratifying: the chemical seems to drain the slugs' oil tanks. Without any lubricant to glide on, they are trapped at the scene of their crimes in a puddle of their own grease. Metameal immobilizes slugs but doesn't necessarily kill them. They may recover when evening dampness restores their fluid. It's advisable to finish the job by snipping them in half or dropping them into a can of salted water.

In severe infestations, Metameal might not be sufficient protection. If slugs come upon primroses first, they may polish them off before they find the bran. Roy Genders in his *The Polyanthus* recommends soaking ground and plants with Slugit every three weeks. It is, he says, not harmful to human or animal life. He also mentions a more potent poison, Slugpest, made by Regional Chemicals of Seattle. This has a 50% metaldehyde content and is also sprinkled over plants and ground. I can't speak for the efficacy of either, but my inclination is to try the easy, dry material first. It's more likely to be used and renewed when indicated.

SQUIRRELS are like water: they flow into any area where pressure is lessened. The population is in constant flux yet its density remains the same. A few bullies patrol their territory while a horde of floaters dodge in and out, snatching a bit of food before they are chased, and always ready to seize on any vacancy. It does little good to remove the resident bosses since you will then be overrun with newcomers. When an individual becomes especially defiant in assaults on bulb plantings, and won't be shooed off by chasing, yelling, and hand clapping, it is certainly worth the effort to live-trap and deport him, but if you live near a wooded area of any extent, trying to thin out squirrels is like bailing the ocean with a teacup.

To protect an experimental sand bed at the south wall, I had a wooden frame made and covered with chicken wire. It effectively kept out squirrels and was light enough to be lifted easily when I wanted to take pictures. In the open garden I covered isolated plants with cages of hardware cloth. Both devices looked peculiar but served my need of preserving specimens until I had photographed them. If anyone has a better method of dealing with squirrels, I would like to hear of it.

2

The Curtain Rises

The first brisk days of October are a call to adventure. The air
is electric with change. Dogwoods and sour gums already wear
scarlet, birds excitedly stoke up for their southward flight, and
the winter garden stirs with new life. Cyclamen, colchicums,
and sternbergias are in flower. Ground covers are studded with
the spear points of crocus buds, each with the furled flower
showing through its translucent spathe like a colored parasol
in a clear plastic case.

The bulbs that flower from September through December
offer few problems. Most of them are hardy, free-blooming,
and permanent. For clarity I will discuss bulbs first and then
go on to the more complicated subject of herbaceous and
woody plants.

Let me emphasize again that all bulbs, and autumnal bulbs
in particular, should be ordered early and from reputable dealers who use botanical names. Worthy plants are sold by their
true names; dubious mixtures and inferior varieties need the
disguise of glamorous-sounding false labels. Unless you know
exactly what variety you want and order it by its specific name,
you are fair prey for the sharpers who offer commonplace material at outlandish prices, or try to unload September-flower-
ing crocuses in November.

This warning is neither idle nor exaggerated. I have before
me an advertisement under a November 22 dateline. It offers
a sensational plant—identified in small letters as Crocus
zonata (*sic*)—at 20¢ each or twelve for $2.00. Two dealers of

unquestioned integrity list *Crocus zonatus* (*C. kotschyanus*) at 50¢ and 55¢ a dozen for delivery in August, the proper planting time. The "bargain" offer of cold storage bulbs is four times the price of fresh ones.

COLCHICUMS suffer from split personalities. In autumn their naked flowers are refined enough for the most select rock garden. Their bumptious *alter ego* takes possession in spring, producing a welter of coarse foliage that would put a skunk cabbage to shame, and then dying off in a prolonged exhibition of yellow decay. The leaves stand almost two feet tall, and as they must be left until they actually wither, they present a monumental eyesore.

Once more it is wise to order by botanical names. Colchicums are sometimes listed as autumn crocus or meadow saffron though the two genera are not even related. The easiest way to distinguish them is by their stamens. Colchicums, as members of the lily family, have six stamens; crocuses, belonging to the iris family, have only three. Unless you are cued to counting stamens, you may not realize until the enormous leaves unfold in spring that your "crocuses" are colchicums.

Since it is the overwhelming foliage of colchicums that restricts their use, place them as you would hostas: in bays of shrubbery, at the base of a hedge, or between small bushes in open woodlands. Colchicums will stand some shade, so the last is perhaps the best choice. Their mauve-pinks combine well with woodland greens and browns and are safely removed from quarreling with salmon pinks in a mixed border.

I once grew colchicums in a try-everything-once beginner's garden but soon discarded them in favor of autumnal crocuses. To me the violet-blues of crocuses are infinitely pleasing, especially with the added punch of scarlet stigmata. Colchicums, on the other hand, hover in a segment of the spectrum that causes me acute distress, as tangible as the shiver that follows the screech of a fingernail on a blackboard. This is a purely personal aversion, no doubt rooted in some forgotten childhood experience, and not by any means intended to put off those who delight in the mauve-magenta-amaranth-mallow-purple range.

As John Gerard wrote in his great *Herball* of 1597, "The rootes of al the sorts of meade saffrons, the white excepted, are very hurtfull to the stomacke, and being eaten, they kill by choking as musromes do . . ." Actually the poisonous alkaloid, colchicine, pervades the whole plant, making it almost immune to pest damage. Rabbits and squirrels leave colchicums untouched but slugs—unless prevented by poison bait—dine on the unprotected bud before it is clear of the ground, leaving holes and thin patches that disfigure the flower.

Colchicums should be planted shallowly, that is, with their tops just below the surface. They like a rich, deeply dug soil with a fair amount of moisture, another reason for planting them in woodlands.

It is difficult to understand why so few varieties of this sturdy and free-flowering plant are offered in this country. The chequered species *CC. agrippinum* and *sibthorpii* are not listed, perhaps due to their reputation for being hard to keep. No such difficulty accounts for the scarcity of *C. speciosum* or of *C. cilicicum* and its rich garnet-colored variety *purpureum*.

COLCHICUM AUTUMNALE is the best-known species, available in mauve and white and in single and double forms. The flowers appear before the end of September and keep up a long display. The white single—at least the form sent out by the trade—is a rather soiled white, not prettily tinted with green or cream but dulled with a faint gray-brown overcast.

The double forms of *Colchicum autumnale* are quite spectacular, so full that they could never be mistaken for crocuses. Their mop heads are far too heavy for the frail tubes that support them, and are apt to go over after a soaking rain. How-

ever the plant is so prolific that fresh flowers quickly push up
to mask the fallen ones.

COLCHICUM SPECIOSUM is a majestic plant, not so
well known in this country as it deserves. The white form is
extraordinarily beautiful. Standing nearly a foot tall on a light
green tube, the great goblet might be mistaken for a tulip sur-
prised without its leaves and magically transported to the October garden.

The English firm of Wallace & Barr list the type, the white
form, and another called *atro-rubens,* described as crimson
with ruby tips. Even allowing for a catalogue writer's license,
this sounds like a splendid flower. All these varieties should
be readily available to American gardeners.

Colchicum speciosum has been frequently hybridized. Its
white form mated with *C. autumnale flore-pleno* produced
'Water Lily,' a full double but of such a dismal lilac-mauve
that I wish the white *autumnale* had been used instead. There
are also numerous hybrids of *C. speciosum* with *CC. gigan-
teum, sibthorpii,* and *bowlesianum,* but my very tepid regard
for the colored forms hasn't inclined me to try them.

CROCUS ASTURICUS heads the alphabet but by no
means my list of favorite crocuses. The type is seldom offered:
I know only its variety *atropurpureus* which had a brief stay
in my garden. My notes say that its pinkish violet segments
were narrow and curled inward at the margins, making them
skimpier still, and were disfigured by blotchy streaks like those
of *Iris tectorum.* I find no further mention of *Crocus asturicus
atropurpureus* and can't now remember whether I discarded
it or whether it returned my withering scorn and took itself
off.

CROCUS KOTSCHYANUS (syn. *C. zonatus*) is reticent
to the point of being almost invisible. The flower is lilac, so
pale and muted that a patch in full bloom has no more impact

than a drift of wood smoke. *C. kotschyanus* has two minor distinctions. It is usually the earliest of the autumnal species, though *C. tournefortii* sometimes noses it out; and its yellow throat is circled with a necklace of gold chevrons, each shaped like a child's drawing of a bird in flight, from which it took its former and easier name.

I once had *Crocus kotschyanus* planted among the arching stems of *Sedum sieboldii*. The pale crocus went equally well with the sedum's rosy flowers and with its curious pink-edged, blue-gray leaves. However *kotschyanus* seeded itself too freely to be entrusted among the rock garden's choice alpines. Demoted to an open woodland, its volunteer seedlings made a modest show above the carpet of brown leaves.

The crocus sold as *C. karduchorum* is in reality a white-throated form of *kotschyanus*. Its correct name is *C. kotschyanus* var. *leucopharynx*. Since it lacks the redeeming yellow throat and gold circlet of the type, it sounds too insipid to be worth considering.

CROCUS LAEVIGATUS FONTENAYI is the latest autumnal crocus and ranks among the finest. It is a chunky little flower, 2″ across but only 1½″ tall. Doubtless on its native Greek mountainsides it has to grow only tall enough to top the winter-leveled grasses. Its habit of midwinter flowering gives *C. laevigatus fontenayi* importance far beyond its size.

Within, *Crocus laevigatus fontenayi* is pale lavender. The throat and stubby brushlike stigmata are deep yellow, and the conspicuous anthers white. The reverse of the outer segments carries the crocus's identification mark: a gray-white ground boldly striped with three royal purple feathers, a pattern as unique as a fingerprint.

The tufty, oddly light green leaves of *Crocus laevigatus fontenayi* appear early in November but the flowers dally until just before Thanksgiving. If the weather is at all possible, *laevigatus fontenayi* will bloom through December and sometimes well into January. Heavy snow will of course crush any flowers above ground but a period of thaw brings others bubbling up to take their place.

The earlier crocuses can hold their own in the open garden. Because of its late flowering, *laevigatus fontenayi* deserves a south wall to amplify the thin winter sunshine, and a raised position to escape bruising by ground winds.

CROCUS LONGIFLORUS is a superlative flower, outstanding for beauty, long flowering period, and total indifference to weather. Although native to southern Italy, Sicily, and Malta, *C. longiflorus* is quite hardy and increases generously.

The leaves of *Crocus longiflorus* are in evidence by mid-October, with flowers opening in the first days of November. The name *longiflorus* does it less than justice. Actually the flower is amply rounded: the segments have pointed tips but are broad enough to overlap for more than half their length. Even when the flower is open as flat as a saucer in warm sunshine, it shows no gaps.

The segments within and without are a luminous tint of campanula violet, sometimes marred by irregular blotches or jagged margins. However, profusion of bloom and pyrotechnic blaze of color compensate for careless grooming. In bold contrast to the violet cup, the tangerine throat is set with yellow anthers and capsicum red stigmata, the most brilliant ornaments of any crocus I've examined. The three branches of the stigma are not threadlike but broaden toward the tip in the shape of a horseshoe nail. Being very long and wire-thin at their base, they flutter seductively in any stirring of air, an invitation ecstatically embraced by swarms of insects. Honeybees roughly tousle the flowers in their greed for pollen, while the little emerald-lacquered ones dive headlong into the crocuses' ambrosial throats.

Crocus longiflorus flowers all through November and still

makes a gay patch of color in mid-December. It is available in this country and is as easily grown as it is beautiful. *C. longiflorus* is the species I would recommend most highly to introduce the fascinating art of winter gardening.

CROCUS MEDIUS is the deepest colored autumnal crocus I've seen. The glossy, well-rounded cups are a warm tone of heliotrope, with a blaze of darker purple forming a star in the throat and on the outer surface of segments and tube. The anthers are yellow and not conspicuous, but the stigmata, slashed and fringed on the ends, are fire red, an emphatic punctuation in the deep-toned hollow of the throat.

Crocus medius blooms in the first weeks of November. A native of the French Riviera, it made a good showing in its first year. I can't speak for its rate of increase: by a wry coincidence, both times I planted *medius*, I had to leave the garden before its second flowering. I think I won't order it again.

CROCUS NIVEUS is a white-flowered beauty that lives for me only on my wish list. I have repeatedly ordered it from England but each time got regrets and a refund.

The late E. A. Bowles in his *A Handbook of Crocus and Colchicum* describes *Crocus niveus* as "far and away the most beautiful of all white-flowered autumnal species, with flowers two inches or more in length, a rich orange throat and brilliant orange stigmata which make the purity of its whiteness the more dazzling." Bowles's color plate of *niveus* shows a graciously rounded flower as golden-hearted as a water lily, confirming his praise and doubling one's desire.

Crocus niveus is not a recent introduction. George Maw described and figured it under the name *C. Boryi* var. *marithoniseus* in his *Monograph of the Genus Crocus* in 1886. Bowles rates it as "a very hardy and robust plant which seeds freely" so its scarcity can't be blamed on a weak constitution.

For the first time in my knowledge, *Crocus niveus* was offered in this country for fall 1965 delivery. Now that the long-sought beauty is at last available, it's frustrating to have no piece of ground to try it in. By the time I have another garden, it is hoped that the crocus will increase enough to sell for less than its present price of 50¢ for a single corm.

CROCUS NUDIFLORUS is a dusky charmer, rich purple with scarlet stigmata, and one of the first autumnal crocuses to bloom. It is not listed in this country though perhaps with good reason. *C. nudiflorus* has a curious method of increasing by underground stolons. In addition, Bowles says it may not flower for several years after planting, and then at some distance from where it was originally set. A plant that wanders out of its nursery row may understandably be difficult to grow commercially. If you find a source for *Crocus nudiflorus*, plant it in a relatively wild area where it can roam freely and not in the restricted frame of the rock garden.

CROCUS OCHROLEUCUS, admittedly only a stand-in for *Crocus niveus*, is nevertheless the only white autumnal crocus that persists in the garden and is generally available. Growing in Syria, Lebanon, and as far south as Galilee, the species must be on the threshold of hardiness yet is able to maintain itself if not to increase substantially.

Crocus ochroleucus is a retiring flower, tall, slender, and ivory-white throughout except for a glowing nasturtium orange throat. If it opened wide, as it seldom does, its narrow segments would give it the look of a bloodroot blossom. The color of the throat is so intense that it shines through the closed flowers and lights the base of even the smallest bud.

For all its air of fragility, *Crocus ochroleucus* is in fact remarkably durable and can weather storms that flatten bigger and softer crocuses. The tubes, though slim, are so stiff that the flowers' only concession to wind is a taut quivering throughout their length, a motion quite different from the swaying and nodding of heavy-headed flowers like *Crocus speciosus*.

Crocus ochroleucus is so slight that I dismissed it on first glance as not worth describing. It was not until I had studied it through a camera, that invaluable sharpener of perception, that I came to appreciate *ochroleucus's* refinement. Its outline has a sinuous flow as willowy as that of a Chinese goddess whose crescent pose recalls the tusk she was carved from. Even so, if someone asked, "Whatever do you see in *that* wispy thing?" I'd be hard put to it to defend my liking.

Crocus ochroleucus flowers in November. Its delicacy enhances the stained-glass radiance of *C. medius* so the two make an agreeable pair. *Medius* blooms naked while *ochroleucus's* foliage is late and sparse. Both look better above a restrained carpeter like creeping thyme or *Veronica repens*.

CROCUS PULCHELLUS is related to *C. speciosus* but differs in having white anthers instead of yellow. I have ordered *pulchellus* several times from England and Holland but each time the telltale yellow anthers proved that I had been sent the commoner and more prolific *speciosus* instead.

According to Louise Beebe Wilder in *Adventures with Hardy Bulbs*, *Crocus pulchellus* is lilac and almost without veining. The photograph shows a generously rounded flower with broad, cupped segments and a short tube, in every way a tidier and more refined plant than *Crocus speciosus*. *C. pulchellus* is now listed by a reliable dealer in this country and urgently demands another try.

CROCUS SATIVUS, the saffron crocus, is possibly the oldest unmodified plant in cultivation. Since it is sterile, it shows none of the variations of random or deliberate cross-pollination. The corms we grow have come to us unchanged over the centuries, perhaps actual divisions of the plant whose fragrance delighted the lovers in the song called Solomon's: "Spikenard and saffron; calamus and cinnamon, with all trees of frankincense."

Saffron, the dried stigmata of *Crocus sativus*, was prized in Elizabethan England as a flavoring, scent, pigment, and above all as a medicine. Since the crocus was difficult to grow in the moist English climate, there was never enough to meet the demand. Scarcity and high price combined to endow saffron with magical healing powers—far greater, of course, than common cottage garden herbs such as digitalis, stramonium, and poppy. Gerard recommended saffron to cure consumption, pestilence, weak hearts, eyes, ears—among other ills— and, anticipating the mood-changing drugs, declared that saffron "maketh the sences more quick and lively, shaketh off heavie and drowsie sleepe, and maketh a man merrie."

Alas for legend! Saffron's medicinal properties are pure fantasy. Inert though it is, saffron was nevertheless of enormous benefit to the sick. By the use of saffron, patients were spared more barbarous doses.

The origin of the cultivated saffron is lost in antiquity. It is thought to be derived from wild forms found in Greece and Asia Minor. If seedlings with extra-long stigmata were selected for propagating, the process should in time produce a freak like *Crocus sativus*. Centuries of increase by division rendered the plant sterile. As early as 1629 John Parkinson wrote in *Paradisi in Sole*: "I never heard that ever it gave seede with any."

Despite its proud literary and historical legacy, *Crocus sativus* is a poor garden plant, neither permanent nor freeblooming. The flowers are a rather dingy shade of red-purple overlaid with heavy veining. *C. sativus's* one distinction is its flamboyant scarlet stigmata, longer than the segments and lolling over their edge.

I once tried saffron in a lobster dish. The color was magnificent but the delicate lobster flavor was obscured by a pollen-y overtone like the odor of dandelion blossoms. Gerard confirms my impression, describing the stigmata as having "a strong smell when they be dried, which doth stuffe and trouble the head." If this was a contemporary opinion, it is hard to understand why saffron was so highly esteemed in cooking. Before refrigeration, it was necessary to mask the taste of half-spoiled meat with pepper and strong spices. Saffron however was mostly used in cakes and confections, much as we use vanilla—that is, it was used for its flavor and not to cover a worse taste. Saffron cakes are still popular in Cornwall but, according to Bowles, prove so distasteful to visitors that a special, artificially colored brand is baked for the tourist trade. The forthright flavor of saffron, to the modern taste, seems most acceptable in robust, tomato-based Spanish cooking.

CROCUS SPECIOSUS and its varieties are the largest species and surely the gaudiest. The naked flowers, appearing towards the end of September, may measure over 4" across when fully extended. Held on limber 6" stems, the flowers are in constant motion, weaving and bowing in the slightest breeze. Photographing them would challenge a snake charmer: just as you get them gracefully posed, a breath of wind will swing them round with their backs to the camera.

The typical *Crocus speciosus* is pale blue-violet so closely veined with darker color that it appears almost blue. The throat is light yellow, the anthers gold; and the stigmata, divided into many long threads, are deep orange or even vermilion in some varieties.

After pollination, the tubes of *Crocus speciosus* go limp and drop the huge flowers on the ground where they loll about in a thoroughly abandoned way. Their seductive pose and the theatrical clash of violet and flame remind me of the orgiastic scene in *Scheherazade* when the dusky slaves are released into the harem. A tidy gardener might try instilling discipline by growing *Crocus speciosus* through a twiggy shrub—

a dwarf erica or the prostrate broom *Cytisus kewensis*— but I have an idea that the crocus's innate talent for disorder would manage to shrug off any attempt at constraint.

Crocus speciosus increases rapidly both by division and by seed. Either method may account for the fact that corms bearing the label of a fine named variety, or of a rarer species such as *C. pulchellus*, turn out to be plain old *speciosus*. In charity it is possible that free seeding or careless cultivation might lead to mixed stocks, but in that case at least some of the batch should be true to name. When *speciosus* is repeatedly sent out in place of its betters, it is hard to believe that the substitution is accidental.

Whatever the cause, the result is confusion. With distinct species such as *pulchellus*, the error is at once obvious. Varieties within a species, however, differ mainly in size or color. These superficial distinctions are not dependable, varying as they do with soil and climate. In any case color perception is subjective and difficult to convey in words with any degree of precision. As an example *Crocus speciosus* 'Cassiope' is described in one catalogue as bluish lavender and in another as aniline blue. The fact that there is no such thing as an aniline blue crocus makes identification even less assured.

Whenever possible I have cross-checked by ordering one variety from several sources, with results that sometimes brought more puzzles than they solved. My remarks on *speciosus* must therefore be taken as pointers for further exploration and not as firm conclusions.

CROCUS SPECIOSUS ALBUS is slender, with pointed segments that flare outward at the tip in the manner of a lily-flowered tulip. Its yellow throat and orange stigmata are doubly effective in contrast to the purity of the flower. Unfortunately, as is the case with most albinos, *C. s. albus* is as frail as it is lovely. Its first flowering was sparse; the few blooms that showed in its second year were plainly a farewell appearance.

CROCUS SPECIOSUS 'CASSIOPE'—or at least the superlative variety I had by that name—is an enormous flower, opening nearly 5" across and standing 7" tall, yet so graciously formed that it escapes coarseness. The color matches veronica violet, #639 on the RHS Horticultural Colour Chart: a warm blue-violet, somewhat bluer than heliotrope yet retaining a flush of rose that gives it a lively glow.

'Cassiope' is amazingly prolific. When the white tips of its buds appear above ground, as close-ranked as the points of a new box of crayons, they furnish one of the most exciting promises of the October garden.

CROCUS SPECIOSUS GLOBOSUS is described as being the latest flowering variety, dark blue and well rounded. My notes say that it opened several days before the type, and conclude sourly, "Just another streaky *speciosus*, smaller, paler, less lavishly sexed, and not globular at all." The corms were almost certainly not true to name but my disenchantment was so complete that I didn't venture another try.

CROCUS TOURNEFORTII flowers with its leaves in early October. It has the unique habit of remaining open regardless of weather, unlike most crocuses which button up when a cloud goes over the sun. A native of the Greek islands, *C. tournefortii* is a singularly beautiful flower, cool and elegant in form and coloring. The scheme is restrained—light pinkish lavender with yellow throat and white anthers—and might be insipid without the spice of vivid orange stigmata. These last are divided into many threadlike capillaries, elaborately fringed and curled, and so long that they loll over the edge of the flower like the tongue of a thirsty dog.

The segments of *Crocus tournefortii* are pointed but broad enough to form a smooth bowl. The inner surface has a pearly sheen, lustrous without being glary, which sets off the intricate design of the stigmata and receives their equally beautiful shadows. Because the tubes are slightly curved, the flower heads are cocked in a way that gives a variety of lighting effects and makes them a delight to photograph.

Crocus tournefortii is easier to identify than to obtain. My corms came from England, the only source I know. *Tournefortii* is not a rampant grower but increased well enough to qualify as a reliable garden subject. Its beauty merits wider distribution.

CYCLAMEN EUROPEUM and C. NEAPOLITANUM are flowers of late summer rather than of autumn. The leaves of C. *neapolitanum*, however, are so richly decorative that they claim a place in the winter garden. These species, with others less hardy, are discussed in Chapter 8.

LEUCOJUM AUTUMNALE, not quite hardy enough for Zone 7a in its northeastern extreme, is described in Chapter 3.

LYCORIS RADIATA, also limited to warmer climates, appears in Chapter 8.

STERNBERGIA LUTEA contributes a welcome note of sunny yellow to the autumn garden. With 3″ flowers on 7″ stems, sternbergias are in excellent scale to accompany *Crocus speciosus* in its most exuberant forms. The flower is glossy and heavy-textured, with the rather stiff lineal outline of zephyranthes. The resemblance is more than skin-deep since both belong to the amaryllis family.

The bright aureolin yellow of *Sternbergia lutea* is a flattering complement to the prevailing blue-violets of *Crocus speciosus*. At the same time the sternbergia's plentiful foliage, dark green and polished, helps to make up for the crocus's deficiencies in that line. Let me repeat that sternbergias flower with their leaves. An error to the effect that their foliage delays until spring is spreading through amateur gardening literature, apparently copied without question by those who compile their notes in libraries instead of in the garden. Nobody who has seen sternbergia growing could possibly overlook the bold strap-shaped leaves that overtop the flowers.

Sternbergia lutea is a temperamental plant, flourishing in one garden and sulking in the next. It grew so freely in my Manhasset garden that it needed division, yet the same bulbs moped and died away when moved to New Jersey. Despite its erratic behavior I believe that the sternbergia is fastidious, not inherently weak, and so I treat it here instead of in the gamblers' chapter.

Most authorities declare that sternbergias require a dry situation and a thorough summer baking. My experience runs exactly counter to this: the successful colony grew under light woodland shade in fairly rich soil. The blunderbuss technique is recommended here: plant sternbergias in several different situations with the hope that one or more will be to their liking. Make some trial plantings in limy soil, as I have a hunch that excess acidity may be hurtful. Finally, be sure to order in July for August delivery, and plant the bulbs on receipt, putting them down four or five inches.

Woody plants are the main feature of winter gardens in mild climates. In recalling visits to the Carolinas, I find that shrubs made an unforgettable impression while herbaceous material scarcely registered. Camellias and the massed red berries of *Nandina domestica*, various hollies, and tender pyracanthas stand in the forefront, with the inconspicuous flowers of osmanthus, elaeagnus, and *Chimonanthus praecox* supplying undertones of haunting fragrance. With a wealth of large-scale shrubs to contribute flowers and berries, winter gardens in England and our southern states are part of the general landscape, not a specialized area within it.

Unhappily the shrubs I mentioned above are too tender for cold climates. In plain fact, there aren't enough shrubs with genuine winter interest to make a substantial showing in the North. It is this scarcity more than anything else that determines the character of northern gardens, making them differ sharply in form and content from those in milder regions.

In the North, bulbs are the mainstay of the winter garden, which is accordingly scaled down to their size. The few large shrubs that flower in winter can be used with good effect in boundary plantings or at the edge of woodlands. In wild areas the sumachs, though coarse and ungainly in habit, may be grown for the sake of their autumn conflagration and their showy heads of red fruit. The fruit is not relished by birds and is usually left untouched for most of the winter. For this reason it is available as emergency food to save robins and other early migrants from starvation in periods of heavy snow. Barberries and Japanese hollies, shrubs better adapted to cultivated areas than sumachs, also provide a valuable reserve of food, scorned in fall but eagerly sought in the lean days of late winter. The shrubs I have mentioned are of course landscape subjects, not suitable for the winter rock garden with its emphasis on small bulbs.

No matter how long their season of bloom, bulbs are essentially transitory. In their dormant period, their sites can be covered only with the most frugal carpeting plants. Dwarf shrubs are needed as well, both to give a feeling of stability and to relieve the flatness of bulb plantings.

Evergreen shrubs are particularly valued in the winter garden. Dwarf conifers are sedate tenants, showing little change throughout the seasons and therefore not primarily winter subjects. Shrubs that have some special attraction in winter, whether of bloom, fruit, or foliage color, claim an assured place. Those suitable for the rock garden can be counted on your thumbs.

BERBERIS VERRUCULOSA compresses a great deal of individuality into a small frame, with far more appeal than its common name of warty barberry implies. Its stubby branches arch and bend to the ground to form a natural bonsai. The thickly set leaves, glossy dark green with a silvery reverse, conceal three-way spines sharp enough to command extreme wariness when you work nearby.

The little barberry is hung with bright yellow flowers in May, an added dividend though outside the focus of this work. The blue-black fruits are not conspicuous. The barberry's contribution to the winter garden lies in a striking pattern of foliage color. In November some of its leaves turn shining scarlet while the rest remain green, for all the world as if some wag had been playing tricks with a bottle of red nail polish. As the cold deepens, the red leaves regain some of their green and the green ones redden, so that the plant eventually goes through the rest of the winter in a fairly uniform shade of bronzy russet.

Berberis verruculosa is evergreen to about zero. Below that, if there is no snow cover, it will lose most of its leaves and probably some terminal twigs as well. If the dead tips are pruned away—and make sure your garden gloves have no holes or thin places before you operate—new growth will quickly replace the damage. After a mild winter you may want to cut back overvigorous upright shoots to keep the bush small and low.

CALLUNAS, the true heathers, are subject to winter burn in snowless seasons and are therefore unsuited to the concentrated sunshine of the winter garden. Further comments on callunas will be found in the notes on *Erica carnea* in this chapter.

CAMELLIAS suffer from a popular misconception. *Camellia sasanqua* varieties are smaller flowered and generally less desirable than the *japonicas*. Apparently because they are common and coarse-growing, *sasanquas* are considered hardier. In actual test, exactly the reverse is true. *Sasanquas* are browned at 10° and killed outright at zero. Even if the shrubs themselves were hardy, their flowers appear in late November and are scattered like pink and white confetti by inevitable frosts.

November-flowering *Camellia japonicas* fail in the North for the same reason. Their partly opened buds and flowers are a little more resistant to cold, going as low as 25° without injury. However, their maddeningly deliberate term of expanding, which may extend over a period of weeks, puts them in almost certain peril of being turned to dry husks by more severe cold. In the mild Carolinas and farther south, camellias are one of the glories of the winter garden. North of Washington, the only camellias that have a sporting chance of flowering well are the latest varieties, those that bloom in April when danger of frost is past. This puts camellias outside the category of winter-flowering shrubs in cold climates.

CHIMONANTHUS PRAECOX typifies a familiar problem: it is a hardy shrub with tender flowers. Though it grew in a garden I visited frequently, I never saw it in fragrant bloom. Since the limp rags of frozen flowers are anything but attractive, I regretfully relinquish any likelihood of enjoying chimonanthus in the North.

COTONEASTERS are a confusing tribe, partly because their names are muddled in commerce and partly because their behavior differs so drastically in mild and severe climates. Species that grow rampantly in England and in our southern states are barely able to maintain themselves in the North.

The fishbone stems of deciduous cotoneasters are not or-

namental in winter after birds have eaten the red berries. On
the other hand, the handsomer evergreen sorts are doubtfully
hardy in Zone 7a. *Cotoneaster microphylla thymifolia*, the
only one I have tried, succumbed to its first winter. Newly
planted shrubs are of course subject to heaving by frost in
open winters so one trial is not a conclusive test of hardiness.
In addition I had assumed that cotoneasters, like most broad-
leaved evergreens, like acid conditions. My failure to provide
neutral to alkaline soil may have contributed to the loss.

Perhaps deficiency of lime may account for the poor performance of evergreen cotoneasters in the Brooklyn Botanic
Garden. *Cotoneaster congesta* (syn. *C. microphylla glacialis*)
is said to make a wide-spreading, hummocky mat in mild
climates. The little specimen in the Garden is open and
sickly, with more dead wood than living. The only thriving
dwarf evergreen variety is *C. microphylla cochleata*, a creeper
that has spread most attractively over the coral rock edging,
following its contours as snugly as a liverwort and rooting in
the lime-rich pores. It looks like a vigorous grower, perhaps
too fast-spreading for southern rock gardens, but I believe the
New York climate will work enough damage to keep new
growth in check. Blankets of evergreen branches are used extensively in the Garden, as much to foil a plague of rabbits as
to protect from burning. If *C. m. cochleata* can endure New
York winters with no covering, it would be a superb camouflage for joints in rockwork.

ELAEAGNUS PUNGENS is associated in my memory
with a Thanksgiving visit to Clarendon Gardens in Pinehurst,
North Carolina. As I walked through the grounds I was
drawn by a teasing fragrance, thinning at times and then drift-
ing back so strongly that the perfume filled the air like a fine
mist. I remember my sharp disappointment when I finally
traced the delicious scent to a huge, shambling bush with
rusty-looking foliage and dirty-white flowers.

Elaeagnus pungens was grown in a nursery in northern New Jersey where winter temperatures of —20° are not uncommon. I didn't see any flowers, however, and suspect that they may be as tender as those of *Chimonanthus praecox*. The elaeagnus is certainly not worth growing for its shabby foliage alone. Even if a mild climate assures flowering, the bush should be put in the back of a shrub border where it can be smelled but not seen.

ERICA CARNEA 'KING GEORGE' is without a doubt the most delightful and improbable shrublet for the winter garden. It forms its buds in autumn, begins to color with killing frost, and stays rosy and cheerful until the first warm days of March. In cold fact, when checked with the color chart, 'King George' is magenta rose, a shade that would be looked on with disdain in the abundance of midsummer. In January's gray wasteland, 'King George' appears rich crimson, a heart-warming color especially appealing when set off by powdery snow.

An erica's tubular flowers are similar to those of the calluna or true heather. A difference in foliage, however, affords a sure means of distinction. Ericas have spiky leaves ranged round the stem like the needles of spruce, while calluna's overlapping, scalelike leaves resemble those of arborvitae. Unscrupulous dealers deliberately switch the names, exploiting heather's romantic connotations in order to sell the less familiar erica.

While I deplore false naming, in this case the gardener may gain by getting an erica instead of a heather. Ericas are far easier to grow, needing full sun and gritty soil mixed with a good quantity of acid peat or leafmold. Callunas do best in a cool, moist situation, preferably on a north-facing slope which slants away from the sun. Even so they may burn unless covered by evergreen branches, which outlaws them from the winter garden.

'King George' should be given a crew cut after blooming to

keep it from growing straggly. The erica's outer twigs root themselves and can easily be detached and grown on to flowering size. A good stock of junior ericas will be of value to replace the parent plant if it outgrows its space, and to give to visitors who lose their hearts to the plucky little plant when they see it flowering in the snow.

I have grown other varieties of *Erica carnea*—'Springwood White' and 'Snow Queen' are examples—but found them either leggy or late-flowering. The magnificent *Erica vagans* varieties 'Lyonesse,' 'Mrs. D. F. Maxwell' and 'St. Keverne,' and the *E. mediterranea* hybrid 'W. T. Rackliff,' admired in Carl Starker's Oregon garden, failed to survive the rigors of winter in the Northeast.

HAMAMELIS JAPONICA and H. MOLLIS are treelike shrubs or shrubby trees, liking damp situations and flowering profusely in February. Of the two witch hazels, *H. japonica* is the stronger grower. It may reach a height of 30′ at maturity while its horizontal branches spread to 15′ or 20′. If you have space for it—ideally the bank of a brook in a sunny meadow—*H. japonica* will pay its rent in gold. Its flowers crowd along bare branches like little tufts of crinkled thread, bright yellow with a red-brown calyx. Though they are small, the flowers make a gratifying display of sunny color—and, unlike elaeagnus and chimonanthus, are immune to frost, staying fresh and unharmed even when the brook is locked in gray ice.

The Chinese *Hamamelis mollis* is a finer plant but unhappily not so hardy as *H. japonica*. It is more upright in habit, and though slow to get a start, may also reach 30′ in mild climates. *Mollis* has larger flowers with petals only slightly waved, and of so rich a shade of orange-yellow that they look like ravelings of bright gold thread.

Because *Hamamelis mollis* grows slowly on its own roots, it is usually grafted on stock of *H. virginiana*. All too often the top winterkills and growth starts from the understock. If you find your *mollis* hanging out little straw-yellow flowers in October, you will know that our native *H. virginiana* has taken its place.

IRIS UNGUICULARIS (syn. *Iris stylosa*) is one of the chief glories of winter gardens in mild regions. E. A. Bowles in *My Garden in Spring* gives explicit directions for growing the iris and, when frost threatens, for slipping the buds out of their spathes to open indoors. I felt confident that even if I couldn't enjoy *Iris unguicularis* in the garden, it would at least make a delightful ornament for the house. Once again it proved a case of a hardy plant with tender flowers. In periods of severe cold, the buds were pulped by freezing long before they had developed enough to be gathered.

Iris unguicularis was the one nonwoody, nonbulbous winter flowering plant that seemed at all possible in Zone 7a. Its tough leaves and vigorous growth were so promising that I felt there must be some way to preserve the buds. I tried several varieties in the warmest place I could give them, right against the bricks of the south wall. In their third year I had one flower which opened on December 11 in a freakish spell of warm weather that was never repeated. The flower was quite handsome, rather like a mid-blue *Iris sibirica* with the typical dark-veined white haft and yellow midrib, but on a slender 8″ tube instead of *sibirica's* rigid stem.

The thick, straggly leaves of *Iris unguicularis* are not attractive in themselves and afford a haven for slugs. I eventually discarded the plants, feeling that it made better sense to guard crocuses against slug damage than to wait perhaps three years for a second iris flower.

JASMINUM NUDIFLORUM might be taken at a distance for an early-flowering forsythia. On approaching, you notice that its slender, whippy canes are as green as a broom's.

Closer inspection shows that the flowers, though tubular at the base, have flat faces with broad lobes. They look in fact more like single primroses than like the skimpy, irregular floret of forsythia. Perhaps the prettiest detail of *Jasminum nudiflorum* is the rich terra-cotta shading on the tube and closed bud, an interplay of tone that makes forsythia's uniform yellow look monotonous by comparison.

The habit of *Jasminum nudiflorum* presents a problem. Its supple canes are not quite erect enough to form a shapely bush, nor prostrate enough for a creeper. Though the plant is a vigorous grower, its individual canes are short lived. If allowed to grow untended, the jasmine soon becomes a jumbled thicket of unsightly dead canes. It should be kept open enough to be easily pruned, but by no means clipped into a formal hedge: it loses all its willowy grace when chopped back to stiff stubs.

I grew *Jasminum nudiflorum* along a wall top, pinning a few main stems down with stones and letting the long shoots trail down the wall face. This made a charming picture but the restricted growth didn't provide enough stems to cut for the house. In *My Garden in Autumn and Winter*, Bowles suggests an ingenious method for handling the jasmine: "It makes quite a pleasing bush if trained round three central sticks and cut back each Spring after flowering, and then allowed to push out new growths in every direction. These make better shoots for cutting than one can get from plants trained on walls . . ."

Where space is limited, *Jasminum nudiflorum* can be tied against a wall as one would do with a climbing rose. Its clear yellow flowers would be charming against a brown cedar fence, and the green stems are interesting in all seasons. Less formally it can be used as a bank cover, but if planted closely enough to keep out weeds, the job of cleaning out dead canes would be somewhat difficult.

The flowers of *Jasminum nudiflorum* are not indestructible

and will be injured by severe frost, yet there are always enough buds to flicker out on the next mild day. If I appear to be inconsistent in recommending a tender-flowered shrub for the North, it's because the plant doesn't look distressed. Frosted flowers drop off cleanly and the green stems are always healthy and pleasant to look at.

LONICERA FRAGRANTISSIMA is a leggy shrub with no pretension to beauty of form, leaf, or bloom—a flowering brush heap, in the apt phrase of my landscape architect, Nelva Weber. *Lonicera fragrantissima* has no merit aside from its sweet scent—and this has little value in the North because the shrub flowers in the raw days of early March.

As it happens, almost all the highly perfumed shrubs flower in the North before it is warm enough to sit outdoors or even to leave windows open for the scent to drift in. There seems little reason for rushing the season with a homely shrub like *Lonicera fragrantissima* since it adds nothing to the landscape when seen from the house. It is better economy to use the space for mock oranges, lilacs, and tree wistaria, beautiful enough to cut for leisurely enjoyment indoors. As far as outdoor fragrance goes, I'd be content to wait until late April for *Viburnum carlesii*, a delight both for its pink and white, arbutuslike flower clusters and for its intoxicating scent. At this time, garden work is in full swing. It's warm enough to spend most of the day outdoors as long as you keep moving briskly, and sheer bliss to pass and return through clouds of the viburnum's spicy fragrance.

PRUNUS SUBHIRTELLA AUTUMNALIS, the autumn cherry, can be grown either as a standard or a shrub. When trained to a single trunk, the prunus will make a 20′ tree with a flat top and somewhat pendulous twigs. As a many-stemmed shrub it will provide more branches for cutting but I think the tree form is prettier. The small white flowers look their best when seen from below against a blue sky.

Prunus subhirtella autumnalis starts to bloom in November and puts out a few flowers in mild spells throughout the winter. Its main display—still modest but a little more substantial—is in spring, when the flowers have a becoming tinge of pink. The prunus is not a smasher by any account but has a delicate charm and of course the appeal of novelty. Except for the witch hazels, the cherry is the only winter-flowering tree adapted to growing in the North.

RHODODENDRON MUCRONULATUM blooms with forsythia with tooth-grating effect. Its doleful, soiled magenta is rendered even more revolting when contrasted with forsythia's bright chrome yellow. There is an attractive form called 'Cornell Pink,' a good clear color almost without taint of blue. Like the type, 'Cornell Pink' forms a stiff, narrow bush with no side branching. It should be planted in groups of three or more to improve its proportions.

SKIMMIA JAPONICA and S. REEVESIANA are rated as doubtfully hardy in the North. Based on over ten years' experience, I believe that skimmias have a better chance of surviving than hybrid tea roses. They grew without any leaf burn in Manhasset, in Zone 7a, with a minimum temperature of zero. Moved to Tenafly the plants lost their tips each year and were cut to the ground in the brutal winter of 1962–63—with, I fear, enough latent root damage to keep them from recovering.

Skimmias are eminently worth growing where winter temperatures stay above zero. *Skimmia japonica* makes the handsomer bush, being broader than it is high and densely clothed with glossy, evergreen leaves shaped like those of kalmia. It is really spectacular when covered with clusters of scarlet berries, set compactly into the mass of the bush. The berries are not relished by birds and so last all winter and well into spring, unlike hollies, photinia, and pyracantha which are stripped almost before they are ripe. I grow these shrubs, as well as blueberries, shadbush, and dogwoods, primarily to attract birds, with an accepted loss of ornamental effect. I think I'm entitled to keep one berried shrub for my own enjoyment.

Skimmia reevesiana is a lower, more open plant, on the edge of being straggly, with duller green foliage. While it is not so fine as *S. japonica, reevesiana* seems to be a little hardier. A clump of *reevesiana,* still bright with berries in April, may be seen in the southeast corner of the Brooklyn Botanic Garden's rockery.

Because of its low, billowy mass, *Skimmia japonica* is excellent for facing down taller shrubs that tend to get leggy with age, as do some camellias and rhododendrons. The association is a logical one since all these shrubs have the same cultural needs. They should be protected against winter sun either by standing in the shade of tall evergreens to the south or against a north-facing wall. Since the shrubs are all surface rooting, a permanent mulch should be maintained to hold moisture and keep the soil cool. Pull weeds by hand and never, never cultivate with a tool for this will scrape feeding roots near the surface.

With *Skimmia japonica,* only the females bear fruit but must have a male nearby for pollination. As compensation for lack of berries, the white flower clusters of the male are larger and more fragrant. *Skimmia reevesiana* is said to be self-fertile.

Skimmia japonica (and I presume *reevesiana* also though I haven't grown it) can be propagated easily by cuttings. A terminal shoot freed of its lower leaves and stuck in the ground in a shady place will form a bundle of roots in a few months. In taking cuttings, be sure to include some from a male plant, but label them and keep them separate. In this way, if you give your surplus away or want spare plants for your own use, you will be sure of having berries without an unnecessary number of nonfruiting males.

If you live in a borderline zone, it is prudent to keep a stock of cuttings in a cold frame in case an abnormal winter wipes out plants in the open. In any case you can hardly have too many skimmias. The drabness of conventional evergreen borders—rhododendrons, kalmia, pieris, Japanese hollies, and conifers—is wonderfully brightened by masses of scarlet-fruited skimmias set before and between them.

VIBURNUM FRAGRANS comes into bloom toward the end of March. Its flower clusters, smaller than those of *Viburnum carlesii* but deeper pink, are scattered among leafless brown branches with charming effect. The fragrance is like that of V. *carlesii* and its offspring *carlcephalum:* as spicy as a carnation but with a heady floral overtone. The scent of *fragrans* is, I find, less pervasive than that of the two later-flowering viburnums. Quite probably the aroma is released freely only when the air is warm.

Viburnum fragrans is a tall, lanky shrub with branches that tend to droop. It should not be grown as an isolated specimen. I have seen it well placed behind a tremendous mass of V. *carlesii* and also behind a head-high wall. In both cases *fragrans's* bare shanks were effectively concealed while its pink-spangled branches arched forward in clear view.

A few sprigs of *Viburnum fragrans,* cut in bud to open in the house, make charming nosegays and scent a room with their potpourri blend of clove and rose petal. *Fragrans* may be cut with a clear conscience since its rather straggly form is improved by pruning.

If space allows only one fragrant viburnum, I would choose V. *carlesii* for outdoor enjoyment in late April when noonday heat floods the garden with powerful scent. I agree with Francis Bacon that ". . . the breath of flowers is far sweeter in the Air (where it comes and goes, like the Warbling of Musick) than in the hand, therefore nothing is more fit for that delight, than to know what be the flowers and plants that do best perfume the Air."

3

A Nosegay for New Year's

For winter gardeners, spring comes in with the New Year. The earliest flowers, according to twenty years of record-keeping, are *Crocus sieberi atticus* and the giant snowdrop, *Galanthus elwesii*. The two names are so often linked in my notes that they form a refrain. "January 4: 2nd *Crocus sieberi*, 1st *Galanthus elwesii* by south wall . . . January 29: 4° temperature—*Crocus sieberi* and *Galanthus elwesii* unharmed." Since both are easy, dependable, and inexpensive, I put them at the very top of the list of January flowers—not only for beginners but to form the backbone of the most sophisticated collection.

Later snowdrops and varieties of *Crocus sieberi*, in some cases even more beautiful than the earliest forms, will also be discussed in this chapter. I will include leucojums as well because they closely resemble snowdrops and are often mistaken for them.

CROCUS SIEBERI ATTICUS once flowered for me on December 24. It was my most heart-lifting Christmas gift: a foretaste of spring. The crocuses have never equalled their record but their usual appearance in the first two weeks of January brings excitement enough.

Crocus sieberi atticus is a rarity: a plant so faultless that it disarms criticism. Not a single "I could wish" or "if only" attaches to it. A description reads more like a love letter than an objective appraisal.

In color, *C. sieberi atticus* is a delectable tint of campanula

violet with a sunny yellow throat to warm it. Deep tangerine
stigmata add an emphatic visual punch. Their form invites a
close look with a hand lens. The three branches, slender at
the point of division, expand into trumpets with rippled brims,
for all the world like the vases that top a Victorian epergne.
The segments are almond-shaped, of firm substance, and pro-
vided with a stiffened indentation at the base. This waist-
cincher preserves the goblet form of the flower even in hot
sun that makes flimsier crocuses reflex at a sharp and ugly
angle.

Crocus sieberi atticus is hardy, vigorous, and increases
bountifully. In a few years a single corm will multiply into a
crowding nosegay. The shining, deep green leaves that circle
the flowers are marked with a conspicuous white midrib. Their
exceptional width serves as a means of identification when
bloom is past.

Crocus sieberi atticus was the first species crocus I grew,
and keeps first place in my affections. It came to me from
William Craig as plain *sieberi*, the name used in commerce
today. However, according to Bowles and with the present
backing of Patrick Synge, the name *sieberi* was first applied to
a Cretan crocus, royally banded in purple and white and considered somewhat tender. The Cretan form, once known as
var. *versicolor*, is now established as the type. The familiar unmarked violet crocus must therefore be qualified by the va-
rietal tag *atticus* in reference to its Greek origin. It is still listed
as *Crocus sieberi* but I have used the full name in the hope
that some day, *some* day, the writers of catalogues will enlist
a taxonomist to check their terminology.

CROCUS SIEBERI 'BOWLES'S WHITE' appeared among
Bowles's seedlings in 1923 but is not yet in general commerce.
His color plate in *A Handbook of Crocus and Colchicum*
shows a wide-open, ice-white flower with an incandescent
center. In Bowles's words, "The wonderfully fine contrast be-

tween its pure white perianth with the orange throat and scarlet stigmata is only equalled among Crocuses by the autumnal *C. niveus.*" 'Bowles's White' stands with *niveus* at the top of the wish list.

CROCUS SIEBERI 'FIREFLY' came to me in 1957. My notes describe "a *very* handsome crocus with rounded segments and broad, white-striped leaves. Came as *dalmaticus* 'Firefly' and certainly isn't." The impostor was a sturdy, square-shouldered crocus of heavy substance and a singularly glowing color, mineral violet by the chart, a lively tint of amethyst with quite a bit of pink in it.

I had grown and discarded its reputed parent, *C. dalmaticus,* a splinter-thin flower with pointed segments, pinkish within and grayish without. I couldn't believe that this furled umbrella of a flower had produced such a nobly rounded child, and expressed my doubts to my supplier, P. de Jager & Sons, mentioning that 'Firefly' had leaves broad enough for a *sieberi.* They wrote back that the plant had been identified as *Crocus sieberi tricolor.* This was getting warmer but still incorrect: *tricolor* has a white zone between its violet top and yellow throat, while 'Firefly' is self-colored. Perhaps the easiest solution was to coin a new name. At any rate, the flower appeared in the next catalogue as *C. sieberi* 'Firefly'—I hope on sounder authority than my amateur guess.

By any name, even a tag of expediency, 'Firefly' is a first-rate plant. It is a little larger than *sieberi atticus* but somewhat less prolific. Because of its unique pink-violet color, it enhances any grouping of pastel flowers. I like it especially beside the luscious ivory-to-gold *Crocus chrysanthus* 'Cream Beauty' with the taller, pale blue spikes of *Scilla tubergeniana* set close behind.

CROCUS SIEBERI 'HUBERT EDELSTEN' is the most spectacular of the *sieberi.* Named for its breeder, it is one of the

few man-made flowers on the winter garden list. It is a
cross between the tender, gaily patterned Cretan type and
the rugged, uniform violet *atticus*. By a happy chance it inherits the assets of both: the richly colored bands of the
Cretan parent and the hardiness of the Greek. By comparison
with Bowles's plate of the Cretan *sieberi*, 'Hubert Edelsten'
gains also in greater roundness of form.

'Hubert Edelsten' is a small flower, standing no higher than
2", but it makes up in fantastic color pattern what it lacks in
inches. The sepals are the saturated red-purple of a glass of
grape jelly set on a sunny windowsill. The color is intensified
by a white chevron that cuts a broad arc across the upper
half. The inner petals are faintly washed with lavender, a mere
hint of color against which the white band is scarcely visible.
Anthers are cream-colored; stigmata less luxuriant than *atticus's* but even deeper in color, being marigold orange by the
chart. The saffron yellow of the throat, extending unusually
far up the segments, suffuses the heart of the flower both inside and out with an incandescent glow.

'Hubert Edelsten' inherits a touch of frailty with its Cretan
blood, notably in a rather weak tube which fails to support
the flower after it has been pollinated. My admiration for
'Hubert Edelsten' is so great that I like it just as much when
it is lolling on its side. Perhaps I view this weakness with a
photographer's eye. The languid curves of spent crocuses allow fluid compositions, far more pleasing than a stiffly upright bunch. In midafternoon when the low rays of the winter
sun shine directly into the prostrate funnel of the flower, its
golden throat flames with startling brilliance.

I waited over fifteen years for 'Hubert Edelsten' from the
time I first read of it until it appeared in commerce. It ex-
ceeded my expectations and has been a favorite with visitors
at the International Flower Show. When a shy young English-
man asked if I thought he could buy 'Hubert Edelsten' when
he got home, I knew it had been worth waiting for.

CROCUS SIEBERI 'VIOLET QUEEN' falls short of the family standard of excellence. It is a stubby little flower, almost spherical, squat to the ground, and disfigured by frayed margins. The color is a deeper violet than *atticus's* but with a dusty cast that dims its luster. The throat, when the flower opens enough to show it, is more amber than gold. There seems no reason to bother with this dull flower when the other *sieberi* varieties offer such luminous beauty.

GALANTHUS ELWESII is a lordly snowdrop, sometimes topping 10" and with a wingspread of 2" or better. Its leaves are broad and glaucous enough for a tulip but of a much deeper green. *G. elwesii* can be distinguished from the common little *G. nivalis* by its majestic size and by its unique hallmark, an emerald zone near the top of the tube in addition to the band at its mouth. This second green patch varies in size and shape. It sometimes extends downward to join the marginal horseshoe, forming a fork-tailed pattern like the silhouette of a Luna moth.

Since *Galanthus elwesii* is a variable species, individuals differ not only in form and the extent of their green markings but in flowering time. Normally the buds appear in December and open (if the weather is at all tolerable) in January, but I have twice found a nonconformist in full bloom in mid-October.

If a freeze sets in after the flowers are open, the scape collapses at ground level so that the flowers lie prostrate. This is doubtless a protective device to insure the flowers' being covered by a snowfall. The gardener's first reaction on seeing them dropped limp and apparently lifeless is apt to be, "That's the last of the snowdrops!" When the temperature gets above freezing, the scapes regain their stiffness and raise the flowers from the ground. Of course a long succession of ups and downs may leave them a little round-shouldered, but even a bent snowdrop is welcome when it signals the end of a hard winter.

By one of the exasperating mysteries of plant marketing, the kingly *Galanthus elwesii* is so seldom listed that it is almost unknown. Most people, in fact, believe that "snowdrop" is synonymous with the familiar little hand-me-down, *G. nivalis*. When visitors admire *elwesii* in my exhibits, their first question is, "How do you make them grow so big?" It's difficult to make inexperienced gardeners realize that this is not just a hopped-up *nivalis*, inflated to giant size by some miraculous fertilizer, but a distinct, superior, and extra-early species. Despite my painstaking explanation, many still go away saying vaguely, "But *my* snowdrops aren't out yet."

Perhaps at one time the selection was determined by availability. *G. nivalis* was more easily collected in central Europe than *elwesii* in Asia Minor, but this factor doesn't apply to nursery-grown bulbs. There's not even the excuse of economy for buying the poorer species: in an autumn 1965 catalogue, both are priced at 95¢ a dozen.

As is the case with many wild plants, *G. elwesii* exhibits considerable variation in form. Those with long vanes—my children nicknamed them var. *helicopteris*—will measure 2″ or more when fully extended. My own favorites are those with sepals as round and cupped as cream soup spoons. While these haven't the span of the narrower ones, they have a more substantial air and, I think, a look of better balance than the flyaway sorts.

G. elwesii increases rather slowly by division, which in one way is an asset. If it grew into choked thickets as *nivalis* does, it would lose in grace more than it gained in numbers. Its flowers show to best advantage when they stand somewhat apart, so that no crowding can obscure their singular clarity of design.

While *G. elwesii* is restrained below ground, it produces quantities of seed in capsules the size of Queen Anne cherries.

Seed germinates readily in the open and provides a sure way to increase your stock—as you'll want to do both for its splendid presence in the garden and for cutting. The majority of early spring flowers quickly go limp in a heated room but snowdrops, in happy exception, last three or four days in water. A little arrangement, perhaps with a few sprigs of birch or alder catkins or of pussy willow, is a pleasant thing to have by the arm of one's reading chair, and rates an appreciative glance at the turn of a page.

The temptation to gather snowdrops for the house is irresistible when the garden offers little else. Before you cut them, however, be sure to mark some of the best with a warning necktie of colored wool. Otherwise you may find you've picked all your favorites and left only the rejects for seeding.

An ideal seedbed for snowdrops is among a woodland planting of the dainty white epimedium, E. youngianum niveum. Its woody tuffets and thickly meshed roots make an impregnable defense against squirrels, yet the plant is neither invasive nor competitive. In late fall the epimediums should be shorn of their wiry stems and persistent yellowed leaves. Free of all clutter, the infant snowdrops will then make a delectable spring picture above the new foliage of their guardians.

The main planting of snowdrops should be in the winter garden, under the main windows of the house where you can admire them without putting on outdoor clothes. Since you won't want to spoil the picture by cutting from your main display, it's well to plant a generous supply in an out-of-the-way place where they won't be missed. Fortunately G. elwesii is amazingly tolerant of exposure. Though it is said to prefer sun, I can see no difference in vigor and increase between those in full sun and others under a low-branched black oak. Uniquely, elwesii is indifferent to the blandishments of a south wall. For many years in my Manhasset garden, the first to flower were at the end of the driveway in the very teeth of the wind. Because of this latitude, you can tuck handfuls of *elwesii* in odd corners: by the entry to cheer the postman on a bleak day, or in the woods where the snowdrops' pure outlines are enhanced by contrast with a dark tree trunk at their back.

GALANTHUS IKARIAE, imported from England, made one gallant attempt to show what it could do in a congenial climate. I liked it both for the ruffled flare at the rim of its tube and for the jaunty, ostrich-plume curl of its leaves. Neither flowers nor foliage proved tough enough to stand a succession of hard freezes, and the plant inevitably succumbed. *Galanthus ikariae* is regretfully put down as a most desirable subject for mild climates only, but not for the severe cold of New York winters.

GALANTHUS NIVALIS is the commonly grown snowdrop, an inferior sort with narrow leaves and sepals hardly better than slivers, and with a meager crescent of green on the inner, tubelike petals. Its only merit, in my admittedly prejudiced opinion, is that it grows and seeds freely in shady places where nothing better will grow. Since it is smaller and as much as two months later than G. *elwesii*, there seems little reason to waste garden room on a second-rate species.

GALANTHUS NIVALIS ATKINSII, like G. *ikariae*, was ordered from England chiefly on the basis of Bowles's high praise. He describes *atkinsii* as being over a foot tall. In my cold garden it made a sadly pinched showing and then collapsed, its flower scape turned to watery pulp by two or three frosts. On the evidence of one trial, *atkinsii* appeared to be less hardy than *ikariae*, too tender even to evaluate. Further experiments must be left to gardeners in warm regions.

GALANTHUS NIVALIS 'SAMUEL ARNOTT' is such a superlative flower that it is hard to credit spindly little *nivalis* with sole parentage. Like *nivalis*, 'Samuel Arnott' has only one green area, a chevron that outlines the little snick at the edge of each petal above a neat white margin. Resemblance to *nivalis* is confined to this single green mark and to 'Samuel Arnott's' leaves, too short and narrow in their early stage to balance the large flower they embrace.

'Samuel Arnott' is cut with a lavish hand. The inner segments are broader and more flaring than those of *elwesii*, in fact more nearly bell-shaped than tubular, and are lined inside with green stripes. However charming its starched petticoat may be, 'Samuel Arnott's' special beauty derives from its graciously rounded sepals. The play of light and shadow on their smooth surface has a sculptural quality. A faint crystalline shimmer heightens their likeness to marble.

'Samuel Arnott' stands from 6″ to 8″ tall, opening rather small and increasing in size and stature during the long weeks of its reign in the garden. The largest I've measured was 2⅜″ across when the wings were flattened against a ruler but this is over the average dimension. The leaves at first expose too much bare scape but grow tall enough to match the flower as it matures. The center of the leaf is dusted with a silvery bloom which shades off into quite deep blue-green at the margins.

'Samuel Arnott' has a strangely misted pedigree. It seems incredible that such an outstandingly fine plant could have drifted into the world without a word of notice, yet its origin and breeding remain a mystery. If 'Samuel Arnott' had resulted from open pollination—as would be likely in an amateur's garden—there would be no certainty as to its pollen parent but the seed parent might possibly have been noted. I felt that the RHS would have information if any exists. The reply to my inquiry reads in part: "Samuel Arnott was provost of Dumphries and sent this snowdrop to the late H. J. Elwes who was a well known and distinguished gardener in the earlier part of the century. He gave it the name of 'Arnott's Seedling' and distributed it under that name but there is no certainty that Arnott himself raised it."

It's not even agreed whether 'Samuel Arnott' is a hybrid or a variant of *nivalis,* something that might be determined by means of a chromosome count. For my part, I like to think that 'Samuel Arnott' may trace its superior beauty to a strain of royal blood. Certainly its price is regal. I know of no source for 'Samuel Arnott' in this country but it may be had in England. It is worth any trouble to possess. I have a flower before me as I write and feel that no words of praise can do full justice to its beauty.

LEUCOJUMS and snowdrops both belong to the amaryllis family but only one species, *Leucojum vernum,* is likely to be mistaken for a snowdrop. I will discuss *L. vernum* first while snowdrops are still fresh in mind.

LEUCOJUM VERNUM blooms in early March with the last snowdrops. Though kissing cousins, they make poor companions and are best kept apart. The leucojum's leaves are abundant and of a conspicuous glossy green, too bold to go well with the snowdrops' modest, gray-powdered foliage. *L. vernum's* flower is heavier and more assertive, even tending to be chubby. While snowdrops have three wingy sepals to lend them airy grace, the leucojum's six segments are identical, fat in the middle and narrowing at the end. The points are slightly drawn in below the swelling curve of the flower, giving it the shape of a globose bell. While snowdrops have green markings on the three inner, tubelike petals only, all six segments of the leucojum are tipped with a green or yellow fingernail.

Leucojum vernum is a difficult plant to establish, disliking

The yellow cups and ample foliage of *Sternbergia lutea* provide an ideal complement for October-flowering *Crocus speciosus* varieties.

Crocus ochroleucus, blooming in mid-November, is enhanced by a mossy carpet of *Minuartia verna caespitosa*.

Crocus longiflorus is a brilliant ornament
for the late November garden.

Narcissus asturiensis, under 3″ in height,
is sturdy enough to weather a March snowstorm.
The carpeting plant is *Aubrieta deltoidea*.

2

Galanthus nivalis 'Samuel Arnott'
is a rare and beautiful snowdrop,
worth its weight in the pearls it resembles.

The hybrid *Eranthis tubergenii* is a vigorous
and distinctive plant, easier to grow and to keep
than either of its wild parents.

Narcissus bulbocodium romieuxii, a native of Mt. Atlas,
is an enticing gamble for adventurous northern gardeners.

Galanthus elwesii
shows its regal proportions
to best advantage when outlined
against a dark tree trunk.

disturbance and quite intolerant of long storage. Like *Eranthis hyemalis*, it is best handled as a growing plant. This means begging a spadeful from a well-stocked garden just as the flowers are fading, and planting the block at once, keeping the soil around the roots as intact as possible.

LEUCOJUM VERNUM CARPATHICUM is a stronger-growing plant than the type, standing about 8″ tall and usually carrying two fat bells. It is distinguished by having yellow instead of green spots. To my eye, deep green is more effective in contrast to white than yellow can be. Nevertheless *carpathicum* would be interesting as a novelty if a stock can be located. I have never seen it listed in a retail catalogue, but nevertheless I believe it is important to put the names of desirable plants on record. There is always a chance that some enterprising dealer will take a flyer on uncommon bulbs.

LEUCOJUM VERNUM VAGNERI, like *carpathicum*, is more vigorous than the type and is twin-flowered. Its bells however are tipped with rich emerald green. *Vagneri* is my choice of the *Leucojum vernum* varieties but again I know of no source for it. I have seen it growing in luxuriant clumps with shining leaves and a profusion of flowers, all evidence of good health and generous increase. Unhappily the owner of the garden didn't realize that the plant was in any way exceptional and had kept no record of its origin.

LEUCOJUM AESTIVUM is the sturdiest species but the least desirable. Because it is easy to grow and propagate, it is all too often sent out in place of *L. vernum*. The deception is soon apparent. Instead of blooming in March, *L. aestivum* comes with daffodils and tulips in late April and early May, hanging out a loose shower of four to six green-tipped bells on a lanky 24″ scape. While the effect is pretty in a minor way, *aestivum* hasn't enough substance to stand with the large-scale flowers of the early summer border. *Aestivum* looks far better massed in a meadow or beside a stream where its flowers nod and recover in silvery waves above the tall grass.

LEUCOJUM AUTUMNALE is a fairy's child with hair-thin leaves and scapes bearing one or at most two starry bells. These are white with a delicate pink flush but without the green spots of the broad-leafed species. For all its fragile appearance, *L. autumnale* holds the record for the longest flowering period of any bulbous plant I've grown: a first flower on August 6, the last one fading on October 18. Since the plant is slender in all its parts, it should be planted thickly and given a green carpeting plant to supplement its threadlike foliage.

Leucojum autumnale is just on the threshold of hardiness in the North. Like most bulbs that make leaf growth in the fall, the leucojum was damaged by severe cold and buffeting winds. Though my colony persisted for four years, each winter took its toll, thinning the leucojum's ranks until it disappeared entirely. The bulbs came so close to surviving, however, that I would like to give them another trial, this time in a sheltered place where the delicate leaves would not be bruised by scouring ground winds. Gardeners in Zone 7b and southward should be able to grow this gentle and appealing flower if they give it a warm spot, preferably against a wall that cuts off the prevailing wind.

4

Crocus Chrysanthus: the ABC Complex

Crocus chrysanthus is an enormously varied clan. Its named varieties include some of the finest crocuses in cultivation and some dowdy poor relations. Since catalogue descriptions deal only in superlatives, choosing the best forms is a bewildering task for the novice.

There is a strong probability that the exceptional color range and uneven performance of *Crocus chrysanthus* are traceable to interbreeding with *CC. aerius* and *biflorus*. The case for hybridity will be kept for the end of the chapter for those with a taste for botanical detective stories.

Certainly the beginner has more immediate concerns than plant pedigrees. As a guide to selection, the following varieties—with three exceptions—are rated by their performance in two gardens over twenty years. The listing is alphabetical, not in order of merit. Regardless of their probable bloodlines, all will be found in catalogues under *Crocus chrysanthus*.

'ADVANCE' would head a list of innovations even if it began with a Z. It's a unique color break, not just an improvement on existing varieties. There's no crocus even remotely like it. The outside is basically yellow but so densely stippled with dull reddish purple that the closed bud appears violet. The low-keyed exterior gives no hint of the brilliance within: a strong tawny yellow with a curious matte finish quite unlike the satiny gloss of most crocuses. The widely fringed stigmata are persimmon orange, highlighted along their fluted edge with paler gold in a shimmering radiance that suggests incandescent metal.

'Advance' would open flat to its full 2″ width if it had room, but the flowers crowd so thickly on their short tubes that some segments interfere and stand upright, showing their outer surface. The intermingling of violet and yellow is so startling that it seems at first glance to be a mixture of two varieties and not the bicolored dress of a single crocus.

'BLUE BEAUTY' poses a paradox. The name *chrysanthus* means "gold flower." Blue tones are thought to come from hybridizing with *Crocus aerius* which, in Bowles's words, "is not a very robust species and is apt to die out." It appears that *aerius* must transmit poor staying power along with its blue blood: in my experience, all-blue *chrysanthus* varieties have proved less vigorous and enduring than the typical yellow forms.

For the record, 'Blue Beauty' is a small flower closely resembling Maw's plate of *Crocus aerius*: soft flax blue with a darker blaze on the sepals which intensifies the blueness of the closed flower. Open or closed, 'Blue Beauty' is a reticent crocus, calling for modest companions if it isn't to be overshadowed entirely. I first grew it paired with *C. chrysanthus* 'Moonlight,' an appealing pale yellow miniature, and liked the effect enough to repeat it in my second garden.

'BLUE BIRD' is known to me only in pictures, since it was introduced after I had left my Tenafly garden. Even though I can't vouch for its performance, it is worth recording as an example of a promising new series of blue and white *chrysanthus*. In all probability these derive their color patterns from the Dalmatian variants of *Crocus biflorus: alexandri* and *weldenii*. These crocuses are white within and either blue or purple without, always defined by a clean white margin.

The blue-on-white coloring of 'Blue Bird' follows *C. Bi-*

florus weldenii, while its generous goblet form reflects *chrysanthus* blood. Since both species are sturdy, their joint offspring have a better prospect of stamina than the solidly blue *aerius-chrysanthus* hybrids.

'BLUE BUTTERFLY' comes closer to true blue than any crocus I've seen. Veronica violet by the color chart, its intensity is heightened by a complementary yellow throat and showy orange stigmata. As round as a marble and not much larger, 'Blue Butterfly' would be a likable midget if it weren't disfigured by crumpled edges, dark and bruised-looking. This defect has appeared over several years of observation and so can't be blamed on a single season's adverse weather.

'BLUE PETER' is another blue and white *chrysanthus* introduced too late for testing. Authorities agree that this is an exceptionally fine variety. The base color is blue-purple, so intensely saturated that the normally white interior and margins become pale blue. According to description, the flower has a yellow throat which must provide an admirable complement. 'Blue Peter' is another compelling reason to seek out a piece of ground to garden in.

'CREAM BEAUTY' is a fairly recent introduction and an immediate favorite. It is a large, generously rounded flower of firm substance, lasting a long time in good condition. By the RHS Horticultural Colour Chart it is Naples yellow, a color as luscious as country cream, reinforced by a purple-brown oval on the lower part of the sepal. A deeper yellow throat and blazing Saturn red stigmata give it high luminosity.

Because of its bland color 'Cream Beauty' is a good harmonizer between more assertive or strongly patterned crocuses. My admiration for 'Cream Beauty' was officially endorsed when the RHS gave it an Award of Merit in 1962, describing it as "certainly one of the best seedlings raised so far." A delectable color scheme, soundly backed by hardiness and a profuse flowering habit, entitle 'Cream Beauty' to a place near the top of the crocus list.

'E. A. BOWLES,' surely the finest of all yellow crocuses, is a fitting memorial to the beloved English plantsman whose name it honors. It is the largest spring-flowering species I've seen, standing nearly 4" tall and spreading 2¾". Except when forcibly flattened out for measuring, 'E. A. Bowles' retains the graceful outlines of an hourglass gourd. Above an indented waist, the cup of the flower swells outward in a reverse curve.

'E. A. Bowles' stakes its effect on unity rather than strong contrast. Its soft butter yellow deepens to amber in throat and anthers, with light orange stigmata for accent. A clove brown thumbprint at the base of the sepals gives a note of strength to the bud. The open bowl of the flower has a light-catching luster that singles it out even at a distance. At close range its suave gradation of color is animated yet always subordinate to the sculptural perfection of its form.

Because of its bright but not glaring color, 'E. A. Bowles' combines admirably with early bulbs, except perhaps for the tiniest crocuses. It makes a delightful threesome with *C. tomasinianus* 'Whitewell Purple' at its shoulder, and a bubbling profusion of violet *C. sieberi atticus* to face them down. 'Whitewell Purple' is smaller than 'E. A. Bowles' but the impact of its intense spectrum violet compensates for lack of size. The colors are so mutually flattering that they should be closely associated—that is, not confined to separate blocks but allowed to stray over the dividing line, mingling where they meet as if seed had drifted from the parent clumps.

'E. P. BOWLES' ranks somewhat below 'E. A. Bowles' in size and in beauty. Its coloring is stronger but less refined: a rather ordinary chrome yellow heavily shaded with sepia feathering. The flower stays closely furled on cold or overcast days and is slow to respond even when the temperature gets above freezing. Since gray days are common in February, 'E. P. Bowles' should be planted closely if it is to make any effect in the garden. Because of its curious reluctance to open, it is one of the very few crocuses that will last a day or two in a heated room.

'GOLDILOCKS' resembles a stemless buttercup in color and glossy finish, though its rounded segments have far more substance, being as stiff as plastic and nearly as durable. 'Goldilocks' has an eccentricity that sets it apart from all other crocuses: it frequently produces double flowers, especially in the first year after planting. Curiously enough, George Barr, the originator of 'Goldilocks,' wrote that he had never seen a double and thought the freak must be due to some peculiarity of my soil. P. de Jager, however, reported the occurrence of doubles in his growing fields and confirmed my observation of variants with ten and twelve segments.

'Goldilocks' is an assertive golden yellow. A patch in full sun commands attention and registers emphatically on color slides to the disadvantage of more subtle tones. Soft colors are restful and should predominate but an all-pastel garden lacks punch. Strong accents like 'Goldilocks' add excitement and, when carefully spaced, serve to draw the eye along a border. Their hot orange-yellows can be tamed somewhat by isolation in a green buffer zone: a carpet of *Arabis sturii*, for example, backed by a dwarf evergreen like *Berberis verruculosa*, or in a bay between ericas.

'LADY KILLER' makes little stir in the garden despite its bragging name. It is a spare flower with long, oval segments, seldom opening wide, and not profuse enough to make a well-filled clump. The coloring is restrained: a pure white interior with no yellow in the throat to warm it; outer segments blue-purple with a thin white margin; ivory anthers and orange stigmata.

Except for its black-barbed, near-white anthers, 'Lady Killer' could have posed for the color plate of *Crocus biflorus alexandri* in Bowles's *Handbook*. This puzzling resemblance prompted an inquiry into the status of the species *chrysanthus* which I will defer to the end of the chapter. While 'Lady Killer' pointed the way to many fine dusty hours among old books, I'm compelled to say that it has more value as a question raiser than as a garden ornament.

'MOONLIGHT' is as appealing as its name. Its dainty flowers are light yellow paling to ivory at the tips, giving the effect of a translucent sea shell. The sepals carry an olive-brown blotch extending into a slender flame of dahlia purple, but the inner bowl is unmarked. 'Moonlight' is among the most prolific of crocuses. Fresh buds fill the center as fast as the spent flowers decline, ringing the clump in a gentle curve of resignation that recalls Pavlova's Dying Swan.

Because of its compactness and uncompetitive color, 'Moonlight' makes a charming picture with blue crocuses. I like it also interplanted with the early bulbous irises such as *Iris histrioides major* and its hybrid with *reticulata*, 'Harmony.' The former blooms naked while 'Harmony' has only a trace of leaf tips to hide its bare shanks. Both look better for borrowed clothing; their dark-toned flowers show to greater effect above light yellow crocuses than against wet earth.

'Moonlight' has one fault: as it nears the close of its flowering time, its leaves grow quite long, thrusting up through the clump in a decidedly whiskery way. Still, the crocus is so neatly groomed through most of its life that I can forgive it a little untidiness at the end.

'MORNING STAR' is a pleasant little crocus, not a world beater by any means but a good conciliator between stronger colors. The interior is white with light chrome throat and stamens, brightened by orange stigmata. The outer surface of the sepals is light straw yellow shaded with faint gray-purple in the center.

Unlike 'Moonlight' which grows unkempt only in its last days, 'Morning Star' starts off with a bristle of stiff leaves interspersed with its flowers. These detract from its minor charms to such an extent that my notes read, "I won't throw it away but would order it again only for a display-of-varieties garden."

'PRINCESS BEATRIX' is the largest blue *chrysanthus* I've grown, and so handsome that I'll withdraw my reservations about its type if it proves a good stayer. It bloomed quite profusely in its first year but was almost wiped out by the disastrous freeze of February 7, 1963, when the temperature dropped from 44° to −6° overnight. With no snow cover for insulation, the ground froze deeply. Rain later thawed the surface but was trapped by a pan of ice in the subsoil where it stood for days in a lethal puddle below ground. Many crocuses, so near blooming that their buds showed color, rotted off at the top of the corm and could be slipped out of the ground, leaves and all, with the lift of a finger. 'Princess Beatrix' suffered more than average loss. Its mortality rate can perhaps be blamed on a poorly drained site at the foot of the rockery and not on innate weakness. In fairness to its beauty, it rates the benefit of the doubt and a second chance to show what it can do in a more equable season.

'Princess Beatrix' is a somewhat muted tint of aster violet, deepest at the tips and paling almost to white as it meets the conspicuous yellow throat. The anthers are large, deep yellow, and without the black barbs which have long been considered the hallmark of *chrysanthus* crocuses. The orange stigmata are small and sparsely branched. Like its putative parent *C. aerius*, 'Princess Beatrix' has a dark violet flare on the outside of its sepals. If 'Princess Beatrix' can show stamina to match its appearance, it will stand in the front rank of fine crocuses.

'SATURNUS' survives in my notes as a complete flop. Faint purple stripes failed to redeem its faded straw yellow segments, narrow and notched at the end like a silene's. As if aware of its deficiencies, 'Saturnus' bloomed down its throat, insuring a quick trip from garden to rubbish basket.

'SNOW BUNTING' is on the order of 'Morning Star' —pale straw yellow marked with faint hairline stripes outside, and a white interior with dull ocher throat. To my eye, these near-white *chrysanthus*, muted with a gray or brown overcast, lack clarity and contrast enough to make them sparkle. Instead of these rather insipid combinations it would be more effective to group two decisively colored varieties: the bold yellow 'Goldilocks' with sharp white *Crocus biflorus* or its warmer, ivory-tinted variety 'White Lady.'

'SPOTLIGHT' is a lackluster variety, a tawny yellow ocher with widely spaced stripes of dahlia purple on the reverse. It seems to be a poor doer: it didn't make a second appearance, thus saving me the trouble of digging it up.

'SULTAN' is the third exception I noted at the start. I haven't grown it and at present don't know a source for it. My acquaintance is limited to a provocative portrait in Patrick Synge's invaluable *The Complete Guide to Bulbs*. Even after the subtraction of a few foot-candles for the exaggerated colors of the crocus plates, 'Sultan' must be a blazer. Except for a hairline rim of white, the outer segments are rich red-purple in vivid contrast to the white interior. 'Sultan' looks, in fact, like an enlarged portrait of the Cretan *Crocus sieberi* minus its chevrons but greatly smartened by the nipped waistline of the best *chrysanthus* varieties. I am eager to translate 'Sultan' from my wish list to my next garden.

'WARLEY WHITE' is yet another of the muddy yellow and white *chrysanthus* varieties. Its outer segments are more heavily suffused with purplish brown than those of 'Morning Star' or 'Snow Bunting' but the murky color is no more attractive than the washed-out tones of the other two.

'ZWANENBURG BRONZE' closes the *chrysanthus* list *Buck* on a rousing note. Its name does it less than justice. The outside is not the greenish brown of bronze but more nearly the rich maroon of cordovan leather, while the interior is vibrant golden orange of high intensity. The closed flower is almost invisible against wet earth. When the sun warms it, a seemingly bare patch is transformed into a blaze of color.

Because of its instant response to a change of light, 'Zwanenburg Bronze' is tricky to photograph. By the time the sun is bright enough for a picture, the flowers are open so wide that the bicolor effect is hidden. I tried to keep them closed by inverting a flowerpot over the clump at night and taking it off next morning when the camera was set up and ready to focus. However fast I worked, the crocuses reacted faster. I never managed to catch them completely wrapped in their cloak of invisibility. Much as I dislike being outsmarted by a flower, I have to concede that 'Zwanenburg Bronze' is more photogenic when half open. As the red-brown sepals draw apart to show the golden inner petals, the effect is as festive as a chocolate Easter egg.

The field of taxonomy is thickly planted with booby traps for the unwary amateur. I wouldn't venture a toe without the guidance of George Kalmbacher, Taxonomist of the Brooklyn Botanic Garden, whose headlong swoops around the Garden's Library have left me breathless with admiration and the effort to follow his reasoning. The Librarian, Marie Giasi, has been equally generous with her assistance, unlocking cases of treasured old books for my study and helping to track down obscure references. With the splendid resources of the Library so freely offered by my unflagging guides, I can only plead a novice's lack of comprehension if I arrive at a loose deduction.

In view of the technical complexities of plant classification, a clean-cut formula for telling similar species apart is a welcome find for the amateur. Bowles's key has two claims to grateful acceptance: it is written in understandable English, not botanical jargon, and it is simple. "The most reliable characters are the golden throat of *C. chrysanthus*, together with its rounded, more gourd-shaped flower. Nature has fortunately vouchsafed a special aid to the puzzled gardener in providing black tips to the barbs of the anthers in the greater number of forms of *C. chrysanthus* but withholding them altogether from all forms of *C. biflorus*." If it hadn't been for the enigmatic 'Lady Killer' I might never have questioned the verity of this easy key.

'Lady Killer' is the exception that made me challenge the rule. It has a foot in both camps. Its black-barbed anthers, according to Bowles, should rank it with *chrysanthus*, yet its throat is glistening white, its form slender and tapering, and its coloring like *Crocus biflorus alexandri*.

When I turned to George Maw's *A Monograph of the Genus Crocus* for a basic definition of the two species, I found on his plate of *Crocus biflorus* a variety *nubigenus* with unmistakable black barbs. In the face of this contradictory evidence, Bowles's formula was regretfully put aside.

Maw's description of *Crocus biflorus* reads in part, "The annulate species have so little to distinguish them except their flower-colouring, that it is not easy to decide to which species their white forms or albinos belong; I have specimens of a white annulate Crocus collected by Dr. Dingler near Adrianople, which may be either an albino of *C. chrysanthus* or of *C. biflorus* . . ."

Specific rank is determined by morphological differences, usually of the reproductive parts, and not by superficial flower color alone. If there is actual structural difference, it would be as apparent in an albino as in a colored form. Conversely, if white forms are indistinguishable, they must belong to the same species.

In discussing the color variations of *Crocus chrysanthus*, Maw states, "It is impossible to avoid the conclusion that they are all forms of the same species, though I know of no other instance of an orange species, varying with lilac flowers. It is possible that the lilac and tinted forms may be hybrids between *C. chrysanthus* and *C. aerius*, which grow intermixed on Mount Olympus . . ."

Thus *Crocus chrysanthus* merges on the one hand with *C. biflorus* and on the other with *aerius*. Perhaps the most telling evidence of mixed blood is in the color of the seeds. Those of *biflorus* are described as bright buff, those of *aerius* as red, while the seeds of *chrysanthus* vary from buff to red.

Crocus chrysanthus, then, is not a discrete species but a three-way alliance which might be termed an *aerius-biflorus-chrysanthus* complex, or ABC for short. If this sounds like a vitamin compound, the analogy is apt. For the sagging spirits that afflict gardeners at the tag end of winter, what better tonic could be found than a glowing patch of January crocuses?

5

A *Diversity* of *Crocuses*

The first crocuses to reach Europe from the Middle East were a gift of kings—or at least of kings' head gardeners. The courtly titles Cloth of Gold and Cloth of Silver reflect the admiration they kindled.

Most of the historical crocuses show few variations. Four centuries of soft living in gardens have dulled their wild inventiveness. Numbers however are no guarantee of superiority: some of our finest garden crocuses come from small families. I wouldn't change *Crocus biflorus* 'White Lady' for a legion of dingy *chrysanthus* near-whites, while *C. tomasinianus* 'Whitewell Purple' outshines all rivals like a phoenix in a chicken yard.

To the Elizabethans who knew only the drab *Crocus sativus*, the introduction of brightly colored species such as *CC. aureus, susianus,* and the *vernus* varieties came as a dazzling sensation. In our day, with a rainbow span of crocuses to choose from, some of the old favorites have inevitably been pushed to the wall. Since this is a book for gardeners, I will distinguish between crocuses that have a valid place in the display garden and those whose appeal is chiefly literary or historical.

Many species—the small yellows in particular—are inextricably muddled in the trade. For example, the *Crocus ancyrensis* now sent out by dealers bears no relation to the *ancyrensis* figured and described by Maw.

By and large, the minor yellows are of slight consequence

in the garden. None of them can stand beside a magnificent yellow such as *C. chrysanthus* 'E. A. Bowles.' Their value is chiefly that of curiosity—not enough, in my view, to justify the experiment and research needed to unscramble them.

CROCUS AERIUS is mainly known for its contribution of blue tones to the *chrysanthus* melting pot, as discussed in the previous chapter. Maw's plate shows a rich blue-violet flower with deep purple feathering and an animating touch of yellow in the throat. It seems a desirable species yet is seldom offered. Its scarcity bears out Bowles's statement that *aerius* is a poor stayer in gardens.

I know *Crocus aerius* only in dilution. Its hybrids with *C. chrysanthus* are a welcome approach to true blue, yet in my experience they lack the springing vigor of the more typical yellow *chrysanthus* varieties. It is hoped that hybridists will soon hit on a way of coupling the blue blood of *aerius* with *chrysanthus's* sturdy constitution.

CROCUS ANCYRENSIS, in the form I had, produced a great profusion of deep yellow flowers with extremely narrow, sharply pointed segments. It was one of the first to bloom but proved to be a splitter: the corms broke up into tiny nonflowering pips, producing nothing but a thicket of leaves after the first spring.

Synge's description of a small, narrow-petaled flower agrees with my records. Evidently we both examined the crocus currently sent out as *ancyrensis*. On the contrary, Maw's plate shows a rounded flower with—as he quite specifically states—blunt oblong segments, a characteristic which Bowles endorses. The mystery of how Maw's *ancyrensis* has been transformed into the skimpy flower issued in its stead is, pragmatically speaking, no concern of gardeners since neither form carries sufficient impact to rate a place in the display garden.

CROCUS AUREUS is the most westerly of yellow species. Though its range extends eastward to Greece and Asia Minor, the corms that first lit a fire in English gardens came from the ancient Balkan kingdom variously rendered as Mesia, Mysia, or Moesia, more recently northern Bulgaria and Serbia.

Since *Crocus aureus* is one of the few ancient garden plants with a documented history, perhaps a brief digression may be allowed.

Charles de l'Écluse, a wealthy Flemish student, was stripped of his property when he became a Protestant. Turned out on the world to live by his wits, he used them to such good account that he became one of the most renowned botanists of the Reformation. Gerard termed him "that most notable learned Herbarist *Carolus Clusius*," a tribute well deserved by a man credited with introducing six hundred new plants to cultivation.

In 1573 Emperor Maximilian II called Clusius to Vienna, placing him in charge of the newly established Imperial Botanical Garden. Clusius's scope of plant collecting was at once expanded. Instead of relying on his own audacious, singlehanded explorations, he could now press into service the whole diplomatic corps as searchers and couriers. In this way *Crocus aureus* traveled from Maximilian's ambassador in Belgrade—corms and dispatches riding together—to reach Vienna in 1579.

Clusius must have shared the increase of his golden treasure with Jean Robin, keeper of the royal garden in Paris, who in turn passed it on to his friend Gerard in London. As Gerard noted gratefully, "that pleasant plant that bringeth foorth yellow flowers, was sent unto me from *Robinus* of Paris, that painfull and most curious searcher of Simples."

The impact of *Crocus aureus* on English gardeners may be gauged by Gerard's description: "This hath flowers of a most perfect shining yellow colour, seeming a far off to be a hot glowing cole of fire." By Parkinson's time color variations were appreciatively noted: "Of this kinde we have some, whose flowers are of a deeper gold yellow colour than others, so that they appear reddish withall."

In the face of the enthusiasm that greeted *Crocus aureus* on first sight it seems churlish to remark that by present standards it falls short of top billing. For one thing it lacks contrast: segments, anthers, stigma, and throat are all cadmium orange, the anthers a shade or two lighter but not differing enough to relieve the monotone. For another, the form is variable. Some individuals are well rounded, others gappetaled and of thin texture.

Flimsy though they may be, the buds slip smoothly to the surface through a chimney of sheathing leaves. These are exceptionally durable, ripening almost to the hardness of wood. Their red-brown tubes keep an escape hatch open through the soil and, above ground, provide a label to mark the planting even after the foliage has died off.

Crocus aureus is not a flower for close inspection but, like *C. tomasinianus*, depends on sheer mass to make an impression. *Curtis's Botanical Magazine* for 1807 describes the impact of a properly grown patch: "When expanded by the warmth of the sun, they produce a most brilliant and exhilirating effect."

To my loss I have failed to grow *Crocus aureus* in the desired saturation. Certainly it seeds itself wantonly enough. Its patches are thick with infant leaves yet the youngsters never seem to reach flowering strength, nor do the corms increase appreciably by division. Elizabeth Lawrence, a devotee of winter flowers, wrote me that *aureus* grows like a weed in her North Carolina garden. There's a consoling possibility that the plant's grudging performance in the North may be blamed on the climate and not on the grower's lack of skill.

CROCUS AUREUS 'DUTCH YELLOW' is something of a mystery, a garden form which has no close counterpart in the wild. Like *Crocus sativus*, the saffron crocus, it has become sterile through centuries of propagation by division. It seems strange that such a large and showy flower could have appeared in gardens without arousing comment, yet there is no record of its origin nor date of introduction. It was apparently not known in 1623, for Parkinson's statement that "the seede hereof is of a brighter colour than in any of the other" quite surely indicates the fertile wild form.

Casual gardeners who buy bulbs in unnamed mixtures are sometimes puzzled to observe that the deep yellow crocuses flower a week or so before the white, lavender, and purple sorts from the same packet. Few realize that two species are involved. 'Dutch Yellow' gets its impatient blood from *Crocus aureus* while the laggard purples derive from late-blooming *C. vernus*.

As is often the case, 'Dutch Yellow' pays for increased size with diminished brilliance. Its color is less saturated than that of *aureus*, and is further muted by gray stripes on the outside, and sometimes by an overlay of buff or ocher shading.

My partiality for species crocus quite frankly affects my judgment of the inflated garden forms. Though I rank *Crocus aureus* above its giant offspring, I must in fairness point out that 'Dutch Yellow' has brought the first joys of spring to generations of gardeners who may never have seen or missed Clusius's little gold wilding.

CROCUS BALANSAE is a midget with a certified identity card: an exuberant scarlet stigma standing half again as tall as the stamens and divided into six major branches. The tips of these are in turn slashed and fringed to make a spreading brush of from twelve to twenty capillaries.

The flower is less than 2″ tall but gaily colored. One form I

had was Indian yellow—buttercup with a tinge of amber—
boldly marked on the sepals with three mahogany stripes. Another variety called 'Zwanenburg' was deeper orange with
three feathered bands shading between madder purple and ox-
blood red. Maw and Bowles describe a variant wholly suffused
with red-purple on the outside, surely as strong a contrast as
could be packed into so small a flower, but this apparently is
no longer in commerce.

CROCUS BIFLORUS is loaded with charm, individuality, and two misleading names. *Curtis's Botanical Magazine*
for 1806 deals briskly with the matter: "Why this is called the
Scotch Crocus we are equally at a loss to account for, as for
the adoption of the specific name . . . It is certainly no native
of Scotland but . . . most probably of Italian or Asiatic origin . . ." As for the specific name *biflorus,* a corm produces
not a miserly two but four or even five flowers. Synge identi-
fies *C. biflorus* as the old Cloth of Silver Crocus. As *biflorus*
already had the folk name of Scotch Crocus, I'd be inclined
to follow Bowles in attributing the fanciful name to *C. versicolor picturatus.*

The Tuscan form of *Crocus biflorus* has a glistening white
interior with short, rather closely bunched stigmata. Both inner and outer surfaces of the throat are deep yellow, so that
the flower is collared as well as centered with gold. Sepals are
sharply etched with black-brown pin stripes on a white
ground, giving a smartly tailored effect. The petals, unmarked
in the majority of crocuses, carry a wide black band extending
from the tube to the top of the yellow zone.

The segments are oval with somewhat pointed tips and
might show gaps if they reflexed fully. Fortunately they are
restrained by a crisply indented waistline which keeps their
goblet form intact.

Crocus biflorus comes wrapped in even more brown paper
than *C. aureus.* The sheathing scales are so broad and so

tightly bound that they have the appearance of a woody stem. From this the foliage projects at random angles wherever it can force a passage through the folds—an effect that reminds me irresistibly of the coarse brown netting that swathes the potted palms in hotel lobbies.

According to Maw, *Crocus biflorus* "has a wider range from west to east than any other species, extending from Genoa into north-west Persia . . ." A great number of regional variations would be expected from such an extensive species yet few are in commerce, and these by no means the best.

The Dalmatian forms of *Crocus biflorus* are basically white, marked on the sepals and at the base of the petals with shades of blue from the palest silvery tint to deep purple. Parkinson describes some of the color variations of "The great white Crocus of Mesia . . . the bottomes of the flowers of this kinde, with some part of the stalke next the flower, are of a pale shining purple colour, and rising a pretty way up the flower; whereas another of this kinde, hath a little mark or shew of blew, and not purple, at the bottome of the flower only, which maketh a difference." It's pleasant to observe that one of the *biflorus* varieties, a rather small creamy white with purple stripes, carries the name *Parkinsonii* in lasting tribute to the man who noted subtle distinctions and set them down with precision and style.

CROCUS BIFLORUS ALEXANDRI is the darkest of the Dalmatian series, recalling Parkinson's shining purple crocus. My acquaintance with *alexandri* is regrettably limited to a glowing portrait in Bowles's *Handbook*. It shows a goblet-shaped flower, pure white within, glossy purple outside, with a narrow margin of white to rim the sepals with high contrast.

Crocus biflorus alexandri is scarce, so scarce that van Tubergen listed it some years ago at $1.25 a single corm. With such a wholesale price, it's not surprising that retail dealers don't carry it. I can only guess that *alexandri* is a slow propagator. Otherwise growers surely would work up a stock so that this magnificent variety could be made available.

CROCUS BIFLORUS WELDENII is long and slender in form, its "little shew of blew" pale and somewhat grayed. The new *chrysanthus* varieties such as 'Blue Bird' and 'Blue Peter' would, I think, carry the blue and white scheme with more authority and add the brightening effect of yellow throat and red-orange stigmata.

CROCUS BIFLORUS 'WHITE LADY' is a recent introduction and without rival the most beautiful white crocus I've grown. The flower has exceptional substance, the segments being as thick and smooth as gardenia petals. The color however is not chalk white but carries a faint tint of yellow— not the clouded density of milk or ivory but rather a translucent wash that warms the white without veiling its clarity. The unity of tone is emphasized by slight deviations from it: a small area of yellow in the throat and a gray mark, hardly more than an enhanced shadow, in the hollowed base of the sepals.

Thanks to its heavy texture 'White Lady' stands heat well, seldom opening to full chalice shape but rather keeping an incurved lip like a brandy glass. As antidote to its prevailing restraint, the flower sports a delectable bit of frivolity at the center. The persimmon orange stigma divides into three long, stiff vanes which spring outward at a jaunty angle. When a breeze flutters their tips, they look like a company of semaphorists in animated conference.

In its first year 'White Lady' bloomed with the utmost profusion, sending up five or even six flowers from a single corm. I can't report on its durability or rate of increase since I left the garden before its second spring. On the basis of its remembered beauty, 'White Lady' will stand near the top of the order list if I should make another garden.

CROCUS CANDIDUS as shown in Maw's plate is white with red-purple stripes or a slight purple suffusion. The type seems to have been supplanted in the trade by its variety *subflavus*.

CROCUS CANDIDUS SUBFLAVUS is a chunky little flower, apricot orange with a darker base and occasionally some slight freckling. The flowers are nearly globular and crowd so thickly on their short tubes that they might be taken for a cluster of mountain ash berries. Despite its small size, *subflavus* might qualify for the display border if it retained its color. Unhappily the flowers fade to an unpleasant pumpkin buff which dulls the brilliance of the group.

CROCUS DALMATICUS is born to be overlooked. It is just about the most unnoticeable crocus you could imagine. Its strap-shaped segments, furled as tightly as an umbrella, are ash gray outside and seldom open wide enough to show their watery lilac interior. There's no reason to waste garden space on such a paltry thing when *C. sieberi* 'Firefly' supplies a stronger tone of pinkish violet and is a fine square-shouldered flower besides.

CROCUS ETRUSCUS stands over 3" tall, one of the tallest spring-flowering species, and should pair better with *C. chrysanthus* 'E. A. Bowles' than the much shorter *C. sieberi atticus*, if it were as good a plant. I haven't grown *etruscus* in many years but my notes preserve a lively distaste for it. The form I had was pale violet streaked with darker color, not in orderly stripes but blurred as if the paint had run, much in the manner of the blotches which (to my eye) disfigure the lavender form of *Iris tectorum*. The segments were narrow and rumpled-looking, and many showed nicked edges like the perianth of a faulty daffodil. None of my authorities throws his hat in the air over *etruscus* by any means, yet none voices disapproval as withering as mine. I conclude that I had a poor strain and hope some day to give *etruscus* another trial.

CROCUS IMPERATI returns us to the list of superior crocuses. Only the type is listed yet I had two distinct color forms with some intermediate variations. One form was unmarked, rather tender but incomparably beautiful; the other, a purple-striped tawny one, was proof against zero weather and several times nosed out *C. sieberi atticus* for the title of first crocus of the New Year.

The first sort was long and elegant in form with segments as thick as mushroom peelings. Very likely this succulent texture accounted for frost damage when the crocuses, perhaps still on their Neapolitan timetable, tried to bloom in January. When moved from the south wall to the open garden, the flowers were held back for a month and opened to perfection. The almond-shaped segments were powdered on the outside with a silvery moth-wing bloom, cool and receding, almost invisible. The flower opened to reveal a Chinese violet interior of the utmost vibrancy, set with gold anthers and fire orange stigmata in high-keyed contrast.

My notes on *Crocus imperati* record that "oddly enough, all seedlings are boldly striped black-purple on a gray ground." I'm glad to have my puzzle resolved by Bowles who wrote that he had come to believe "that, unlike other Crocuses, *C. imperati* has a habit of varying in its markings according to vigor and seasonal changes."

Just when I thought inconstancy the rule, I ordered a second lot of *Crocus imperati* for my New Jersey garden and got a fairly uniform batch which didn't seed at all. This strain was smaller than the first, with narrower segments and a little more pink in its inner coloring. The outer surface was straw yellow rather thinly penciled with purple-brown. The furled bud, with its bright interior hidden, could easily be mistaken for a tuft of dead grass or overlooked entirely. This drab bad-weather dress, common to many species, must serve as camouflage from grazing animals—rabbits, perhaps, or goats?—to preserve the flower until a sunny day brings out the insects needed for pollination.

CROCUS KOROLKOWII is a jolly little flower hailing from the eastern extreme of its genus, Turkestan and Afghanistan, a region best known for its superb species tulips. I have had two forms of *korolkowii*. One was a rather frail variety, buttercup yellow with fern green spots on the outside, a color pattern that sounds odd but was in fact quite pretty. This is no longer listed and must, I believe, have come from William Craig, as did many rarities not available from conventional firms. Van Tubergen's *korolkowii*, and that of most of the trade, is a sturdier form collected in Bukhara. The interior is cadmium orange polished to a mirror finish. The outside is heavily suffused with dark brown and overprinted with black freckling.

Crocus korolkowii can be distinguished from other small yellows by its numerous leaves, as many as twelve, olive green in color and spreading flat to the ground. Its anthers and stigma are short and inconspicuous, being nearly the same color as the inner surface of the flower. Despite its geographical interest, I didn't think *korolkowii* outstanding enough to order for my second garden.

CROCUS OLIVIERI is round as a pea and not much larger. Its intense shade of marigold orange surpasses even fiery *Crocus aureus* in brilliance. Aside from its minute size, *olivieri* can be identified by the six equal divisions of its stigma and by its exceptionally broad, dark green leaves with inconspicuous midrib, looking when mature very like meadow grass.

Sitting tight on the ground in a nest of thyme, *olivieri's* tiny globes suggest a revised legend, "The Wren That Laid the Golden Eggs." Honeybees work the flowers over with great determination, biting the tip of a segment to drag it open. The flower springs closed behind the bee, hiding it so completely that a second bee will sometimes force its way in. Since the space is a tight fit for one, there follows a furious buzzing and rocking until one of the bees can kick its way free and burst out the top.

Small as it is, I would include *Crocus olivieri* on the list of desirable crocuses for its concentrated color and for the fun of bee-watching. Unfortunately it hasn't proved permanent with me, thinning out or disappearing entirely over winter. I suspect that it won't tolerate being waterlogged, a condition that may occur even in well-prepared soil when a shallow thaw allows rain or snow water to accumulate on a frozen layer beneath. *Crocus olivieri* probably requires the protection of an alpine house where moisture and drainage can be exactly controlled.

CROCUS SUSIANUS is a second lightning strike for Clusius who received it from Constantinople in 1587, eight years after the introduction of *Crocus aureus*. It is tempting to credit the finding of *C. susianus* to Clusius's friend Augier Ghislain de Busbecq who collected in the vicinity of Constantinople and introduced the tulip, lilac, and mock orange to European gardens, but I can find nothing more substantial than propinquity to support my fancy.

The admiration excited by *Crocus susianus* may be measured by its lordly title of Cloth of Gold Crocus. In form and marking it suggests a miniature *Tulipa kaufmanniana* hybrid —slender, almost stemless, and opening flat on the ground like a spattering of burnished gold stars. The outside, all but a narrow margin of strong yellow, is a deep and glossy chestnut brown, or so my memory and slides present it. My notes, on the other hand, record the color as dahlia purple, #931 by the Horticultural Colour Chart. Perhaps the eye may blend the two colors into a warm brown, but would the camera also be deluded? The masterly plate of *susianus* in *Curtis's Botanical Magazine* for 1803 sides with my notes by rendering the stripes a definite royal purple.

There are other disparities which suggest that time, climate, or new strains may have made changes. Parkinson wrote that "the fairest cloth of gold Crocus or Saffron flower, riseth up very early . . ." and *Curtis's Botanical Magazine* declares, in comparison with *C. aureus*, "This is the earliest blower, and seems more easily affected by frost while in bloom." In my gardens, *susianus* is one of the last to flower, not appearing until the latter part of March, so standing more in peril of cooking than of freezing.

One characteristic still holds true. As *Curtis's Botanical Magazine* puts it, "This expands its flowers in all weathers, the three outer segments of which upwards are rolled back and continue so even when the flower is closed in the evening, never returning to a straight position." *Susianus's* distinctive stripes are shadowed by the curling tips, and in any case the flower flings itself wide open at a glimmer of light, so photographing it calls for some trickery. To get both open and closed flowers in a group, some at the rear can be picked and placed in water in a refrigerator for several hours. When the set-up is entirely ready—background in place, a tiny pin holder hidden behind the plant, camera in place and focused—fetch the chilled flowers at a run, arrange them on the holder, and snap the picture before they have time to react.

CROCUS TOMASINIANUS has a delicate air with tissue-thin flowers as ethereal as a drift of lavender-tinted fog. Its ghostly aura masks a voracious weed. It seeds as incontinently as crabgrass and is harder to destroy by poison than wild onion or equisetum. Its corms choke the ground, multiplying by seed and division until they are as thick as the blobs in tapioca pudding. Between its greedy corms and lank, thirsty leaves, *tomasinianus* is quite capable of killing any small plant

it may invade. It is especially dangerous to creepers and sur-
face-rooters like arbutus and dwarf rhododendrons. Its gray-
lavender flowers are not pretty enough to justify the damage
it does when it takes over a garden. It is easier to avoid *tomasinianus* than to eradicate it.

CROCUS TOMASINIANUS 'TAPLOW RUBY' is just the
reverse of its parent, being so feeble that it produces one or
two sorry flowers and then miffs itself off. It is not red by any
stretch of the cataloguer's imagination, matching imperial
purple (#33, RHS Horticultural Colour Chart), then shading from mauve to white at the base. Still, it's the nearest approach to red of any crocus I've seen. It's a pity that the plant
is so weak, as its color in sufficient mass would wonderfully
enhance the blueness of bulbous irises such as the *reticulata* x
histrioides major hybrids.

CROCUS TOMASINIANUS 'WHITEWELL PURPLE' is so
fine a plant that it almost redeems the evil or sickly aspects
of its relations. Like the others, its form is slender, more like
a daisy than a crocus, but the flowers are produced so prodigally that they present a solid block of color: a rich and telling
spectrum violet nearly as saturated as that of the Dutch crocus 'Paulus Potter.' Although 'Whitewell Purple' is smaller
than *C. chrysanthus* 'E. A. Bowles,' its profusion and intensity of color give it such authority that the two make a splendid pair.

'Whitewell Purple' has an amusing way of sticking the tip
of its pistil through the still-closed bud. If this is a sort of advertisement to insects, the invitation is effective. 'Whitewell
Purple' is a rollicking carnival for bees and therefore for pho-
tographers. Nothing carries such authentic outdoor atmosphere as bees at work or on the wing, not mounted or stupe-
fied with drugs or cold as they must be in the studio. Bees are
agreeably tolerant of a foreign nose intruding on their business

of food gathering. I've spent a good many hours crouched over a rockery humming with bee traffic, arranging the flowers with bare hands, and haven't been stung yet—not even when in a moment of complete absorption, I absent-mindedly arranged a bee.

In spite of the bees' activity in pollinating, I haven't known 'Whitewell Purple' to seed. As far as my experience can vouch for it, 'Whitewell Purple' is suited both in manners and appearance to a place in select company.

CROCUS VERNUS is the ancestor of the great Dutch crocuses. On its native alpine slopes it exhibits the variations now fixed in garden forms, ranging from white to purple with endless elaborations of stripes, feathering, and flushes of darker color. The wild *C. vernus* is a plant of high altitudes, flowering late in the season on the margins of melting snowbanks. It is quite unable to survive in a sultry lowland climate. If *vernus* could adapt its schedule to bloom with the first January thaw, as *sieberi* and *imperati* do, it might get by, but it seems unalterably fixed on April and certain ruin.

CROCUS VERNUS 'HAARLEM GEM' is a hybrid with *C. tomasinianus* and a much better stayer. It is a distinctive flower and an interesting compromise between the two parents, with *vernus's* heavy substance and rounded form and *tomasinianus's* pointed tips. The tube and outside of the sepals are palest lavender with a frosty bloom that makes them appear white, while all the interior surfaces are warm heliotrope. Since the flower seldom opens more than halfway, the contrast of colors is quite striking.

'Haarlem Gem' flowers at the end of March. I wish it were earlier. Three months of crocuses are enough to satisfy the most confirmed addict. Even a superlative specimen would fail to catch an eye turned toward tulips and anemones.

CROCUS VERSICOLOR is a variable species easily recognized (except in albino forms) by a unique feature: its inner segments carry stripes or feathers similar to those on the
sepals. The plate of *C. versicolor* in *Curtis's Botanical Magazine* shows a rounded flower of rather dull red-violet, very
heavily veined on all the inner surfaces. The species is now
represented in the trade only by its variety *picturatus*, the old
Cloth of Silver Crocus.

As I had it, *Crocus versicolor picturatus* was a clear white
with narrow purple stripes on the reverse of all the segments.
Though thin and pointed in form, it was quite prolific. My
notes for February 25, 1957, read "One corm now has nine
flowers and buds showing, very good for a first year. Mass of
flowers may make up for narrow segments as it does in
'Whitewell Purple.'" Later I penciled in, "Move to back garden. Needs greenery."

The following year *picturatus* showed only a few flowers.
The winter finished it off. On reflection I'm convinced that I
must have had an inferior strain. It would take a more substantial flower to earn the proud title of Cloth of Silver, and
a more durable one to carry it for three centuries.

Plant collectors of the sixteenth century were impelled to
search for new and potent medicinal herbs, not for mere
beauty. The large proportion of crocus species brought home
by collectors reflects the need to find a substitute for saffron,
always scarce because of the difficulty of growing *Crocus sativus* in England and the Continent.

Gerard, with the scorn of a practical physician, dismissed
his "wilde saffrons" as unprofitable, declaring them "destitute
of those chives which yeeld the colour, smell, or taste, that the
right manured Saffron hath." Rejected by apothecary and
cook, the little crocuses escaped mortar and saucepan to find

sanctuary in gardens. Parkinson, with his perceptive eye, recognized their aesthetic value and absolved them of "any other use, then in regard of their beautifull flowers of severall varieties, and as they have been carefully sought out, and preserved by divers, to furnish a Garden of dainty curiosity."

6

Grace Notes

To listen to a crocophile, you might conclude that the winter garden, like poor Johnny One Note, can blow only crocus, crocus, crocus. By weight of numbers and brilliance of color, crocuses carry the dominant theme. I yield not one jot of my infatuation when I say that their essentially circular outlines would be monotonous without contrasting forms.

The ideal grace notes for a crocus planting are spikes and loose sprays to offset the prevailing roundness. For the same reason, wherever possible a variety of leaf forms should be chosen as a foil for the crocuses' grasslike tufts. The abundant foliage of anemones and eranthis, fugitive though it may be, clothes the ground in crocus season, while the silver-marbled leaves of cyclamen are superbly decorative for ten months of the year. Finally, since crocuses are rich in all colors but blue, the lack can be supplied by supplementary flowers.

By happy chance some of the purest blues that can easily be grown in a humid, lowland climate—delphiniums and alpine gentians being categorically excluded—are to be found in early spring bulbs. Chionodoxas, hyacinths, muscari, and scillas ring the round of blue from tints as pale as starch through gentle blue-violets to royal blue and blue-black. Though the alphabet requires the list of grace notes to begin with a pink flower, the lovely blues will have their rightful turn.

BULBOCODIUM VERNUM, like the phoenix, is *sui generis*, a unique experiment, the only member of its genus.

Its pinkish mauve color and narrow, thin-textured segments suggest an out-of-season colchicum, while the boat-shaped leaves that cradle the emerging buds look for all the world like the old-fashioned houseplant called Moses-in-the-bullrushes.

The segments of *Bulbocodium vernum* are slit to the base, not trimly joined in the throat like those of crocuses. In fact, the flower is so loosely organized that when you pick it, it falls apart in your hand. Crisp and erect when freshly opened, the segments recurve as they age in a rather blowzy way. Louise Beebe Wilder's description in *Adventures with Hardy Bulbs* can't be bettered: it looks "as if it had almost certainly slept in its clothes."

It's hard to account for the appeal of an admittedly untidy plant. Curiosity is a factor, of course. Few can resist the pleasure of having a flower that not one visitor in fifty can identify. Beyond the claim of novelty, the bulbocodium has distinct value since its pinkish color is rare among spring flowers. By contrast, it intensifies the blueness of *Iris reticulata* 'Cantab' and the hybrid 'Joyce' (*reticulata* x *histrioides major*) which bloom with the bulbocodium in late March. Since both irises and bulbocodium require full sun and gritty, well-drained soil with a trace of lime, their grouping is indicated on cultural as well as aesthetic grounds.

CHIONODOXA GIGANTEA and C. LUCILIAE are similar in appearance yet sharply varied in merit. Perhaps the best way to fix their differences in mind is to discuss them together. *Chionodoxa luciliae* is the species most frequently offered but by no means the finest. Its spray of gentian blue, white-eyed stars is charming when first open. Unfortunately, however, the succulent scape quickly grows too tall for its strength so that rough weather will dash the flowers in the mud. Both CC. *luciliae* and *gigantea* occur in white and a rather dingy mauve-pink but the family genius lies in its celestial blues.

Chionodoxa gigantea has fewer but larger flowers, set face upwards on sturdy, arching stems so that no detail of their beauty is lost. The color range is similar to that of C. *luciliae* but in softer tones. However, because of the greater breadth and substance of the flowers and because they are bunched to the point of overlapping, they present a more concentrated blueness than the widely spaced stars of C. *luciliae*.

Used as a mimic pool below *Tulipa kaufmanniana, Chionodoxa gigantea* heightens the tulips' resemblance to water lilies. While chionodoxas can be grown in the sunny rock garden, their color holds better in open woodlands where budding trees throw a dappled shade. They are inexpensive enough to plant in generous drifts and rivers, two inches apart for immediate effect, three inches or more if you are willing to wait for natural increase to fill the gaps. If anything, err on the side of crowding: in a massed planting, the interplay of shading from blue to violet gives the effect of changeable silk.

In an informal planting, random variation is an asset. If for any reason a uniform effect is wanted, it's entirely practical to lift and divide a particularly fine specimen while in flower— but be very sure to dig with a spade, not a trowel, for the bulbs seem to burrow deeper the longer they stand. An established clump may go down eight inches or more though originally planted only two to three inches deep.

One of the most appealing surprises about chionodoxas is that their color, retiring as it is by full daylight, has the property of intensifying toward dusk. I have a good number of C. *gigantea* spilling down a west-facing slope where they catch the last level rays of sunset. On the brink of darkness when even white flowers lose their identity and merge into grayness, the chionodoxa hillock burns as blue as an alcohol flame.

CHIONODOXA SARDENSIS is the only other member of the genus readily available in commerce. It is a dour little thing, its dark blue flowers relieved by only a minute white spot in the throat. Apart from earliness it has little to recom-

mend it since scillas command the rich blues with as much
authority and more brilliance.

ERANTHIS HYEMALIS sits close to the ground on a
ruffle of green bracts, as innocent-looking as any buttercup,
yet endowed by the old herbalists with baneful properties.
The deeply slashed foliage of eranthis bears some resemblance
to the poisonous aconites such as A. *lycoctonum* which Gerard tells us "is used among hunters which seeke after wolves,
the juice whereof they put into raw flesh which the wolves
devour, and are killed." From confusion with this lethal
cousin, *Eranthis hyemalis* derived its folk names of wolfsbane
and winter aconite.

Parkinson was too keen a gardener to let the hazard of poison stand between him and a good plant. He stoutly cham-
pions "some, notwithstanding their evill quality, may for the
beauty of their flowers take up a roome in this Garden, of
whom I mean to entreate in this place: And first of the Winter
Wolfesbane, which for the beauty, as well as the earliness of
his flowers, being the first of all other, that show themselves
after Christmas, deserveth a prime place . . . This little plant
thrusteth up divers leaves out of the grounde, in the deepe of
Winter oftentimes, if there be any milde weather in Ianuary,
but most commonly after the deepe frosts, bearing up many
times the snow upon the heads of the leaves . . ."

Whenever I see the flowers of *Eranthis hyemalis* tightly
balled against the cold, with emerging leaves still crooked at
the wrist, and each wearing a mobcap of snow, I salute Parkinson's acute eye and his blithe disregard for the dangers of
harboring the little plant.

Much as I'd like to include *Eranthis hyemalis* in the rock
garden, I find it does poorly in the lean, sharply drained soil
necessary for most bulbs and alpines. The eranthis prefers a
moist spot—not a stagnant bog but a water meadow or seeping, spring-fed slope. Try it in varied locations: a woodland

hollow rich in leafmold, or under the winter-flowering Chinese witch hazel, *Hamamelis mollis,* with *Scilla bifolia* or *Chiono-doxa sardensis* for contrast. Where *Eranthis hyemalis* is happy, it will seed itself in glistening golden carpets.

As I've said before, eranthis should be kept out of the ground as short a time as possible. The very best way to start a plantation is to beg a turf from a well-favored garden and to plant it at once with no risk of exposure to drying. Failing this, order early from a reputable bulb specialist—not, if you hope for success, from a general mail order jobber and even more emphatically not in paper packets from the 5 & 10 or super-market where dry heat will quickly snuff out their precarious lives.

Philip Miller, who combined good taste with an encompass-ing knowledge of plant growing, has the ultimate word on eranthis—or *Helleborus hyemalis,* as he termed it. "It is prop-agated by offsets, which the roots send out in plenty; these roots may be taken up and transplanted any time after their leaves decay . . . these roots should be planted in small clus-ters, otherwise they will not make a good appearance; for sin-gle flowers, scattered about the borders, of these small kinds, are scarce seen at a distance; but when these and the Snow-drops are alternately planted in bunches, they will have a good effect, as they flower at the same time, and are much of a size."

ERANTHIS X TUBERGENII is one of the few man-made flowers in the winter garden. Though "hybrid" is a dirty word to purists, it is impossible to deny that *E.* x *tubergenii* greatly excels both parents: a better stayer than *cilicica,* taller and larger than *hyemalis.* Since *tubergenii* is sterile, it can only in-crease below ground, and does so slowly but reliably. By the same token, since it doesn't go to seed, the flowers last excep-tionally long in show condition.

Unlike stubby little *E. hyemalis, tubergenii* stands up to 5″ tall on russet-tinged stems, naked at first but presently rein-forced by boldly cut leaves which stay well below the flowers.

By the Horticultural Colour Chart the flower color is Dresden yellow with a touch of citron in the center, a rather sharp tone, too much on the lemon side to be wholly compatible with the warmer creams and canary yellows of crocuses. A buffer zone of blue flowers—*Scilla tubergeniana* or *Hyacinthus azureus*—will keep peace between the eranthis and its less assertive neighbors.

HYACINTHUS AMETHYSTINUS is perhaps the one flower in all horticultural literature whose blueness is understated. Its color is light and hazy but without a trace of the pinkish lavender its name implies.

Synge describes *Hyacinthus amethystinus* as flowering in March and April but for me it has never appeared before late May or even the beginning of June. Hot weather wilted its tall stem and succulent flowers before they were fully open—a case of "How pretty, wasn't it?" When I gave it shade, it grew lank, limp, and pale. It might possibly grow by a streamside, the nearest facsimile of its native, snow-watered alpine meadows, but my sandy hilltop had no running brooks, iced or otherwise. Though the hyacinth increased well, I discarded it after some years: a flower in obvious distress is no ornament to a garden.

HYACINTHUS AZUREUS is one of the most beguiling flowers of early spring and among the truest blues of any season. Its flaring bells, a soft but bright tint of cobalt blue, are intensified by stripes of deeper color on the outside. Closely set on the scape yet standing at a jaunty angle from it, the flowers combine a telling concentration of color with a most appealing daintiness.

The spikes of *Hyacinthus azureus*, seldom more than 4″ overall, appear in mid-March just as *Scilla tubergeniana* is going by, and thus take over the role of providing a tall accent for the cups of eranthis and the last species crocuses. The little hyacinth, even when it increases, is still essentially slender and should be planted closely—two inches apart at the center of the group and feathering off at the edges to mingle with its neighbors.

Hyacinthus azureus is often miscatalogued as *Muscari azureum* though anyone with half an eye can see that its open bells have no kinship to a muscari's close-lipped pout. The hyacinth is in every way the better plant: its blues are unclouded and its manners—except in one particular—refined enough to admit it to the most select company. In contrast to the muscari's sodden mop of winter foliage, the leaves of the hyacinth thrust up with the blue nose of the bud already showing between them, and then take themselves neatly away after blooming.

Though *Hyacinthus azureus* would grace a Staffordshire flower piece, its delicate air is belied by an iron constitution. Increase by division is slow but—in its single lapse from propriety—the little hyacinth self-seeds with great freedom. It's hard to believe that this small charmer could be a nuisance, but if it is grown near plants that might resent crowding—*Narcissus asturiensis*, for example, with which it makes an entrancing pair—it would be wise to snip off fading flower stalks before seed can ripen.

MUSCARI is a thoroughly muddled genus. There is no definitive monograph: reference books range from conjecture to contradiction and often omit the improved horticultural varieties entirely. Since there's no surer guide, let's follow the alphabet and leave questions of taxonomy to some future monographer.

MUSCARI ARMENIACUM is a robust plant, quite unfairly damned as a weed through confusion with the rampaging variety, 'Heavenly Blue.' A height of 8″ to 10″ would rule *M. armeniacum* out of the rock garden even without a graver fault: its hank of stringy leaves that flop around all winter, harboring slugs and mildew and smothering any soft-crowned plant within their clammy reach. Obviously this is a plant for rough places where its bold mass of murky blue can be enjoyed without damage to delicate companions. It serves admirably to face down daffodils and tulips, not only hiding their rather spindly shanks but increasing the luminous effect of pastel colors by its somber contrast.

Muscari armeniacum is often used beneath flowering shrubs but with less pleasing results. To my eye at least, its emphatic vertical spikes repeat the upright canes of shrubs in a jerky pattern. For carpeting effects I prefer softer forms such as scillas or chionodoxas.

MUSCARI BOTRIOIDES is referred to as the common grape hyacinth by Bailey and the RHS *Dictionary of Gardening* though curiously enough it is seldom offered in commerce —perhaps because of its reputation as a spreader. Its white form, *M. b. album*, is a more restrained plant. Its globes are more oval than round and are set rather sparsely on the scape. While it isn't compact enough to carry a solo part in the rock garden, it gives a pleasantly airy effect when scattered through a myrtle bank cover in full sun.

MUSCARI 'CANTAB' is listed by Synge as a variety of *M. armeniacum*. Both have broad-shouldered, densely packed spikes and are vigorous growers. Despite its size, 'Cantab' falls short of being a striking garden ornament. Its dusty light blue is too muted to contrast effectively with the strong, clear colors of tulips and daffodils. Nevertheless 'Cantab' is a welcome departure from the funereal hues of its common relatives and should be of great interest to hybridists. If crossed with the brilliantly blue but frail *M. tubergenianum*, the offspring might gain clarity of color while keeping the *armeniacum* stamina.

MUSCARI 'HEAVENLY BLUE' was first laid at the door of *M. conicum* and now is blamed on *M. armeniacum*. Perhaps dubious paternity accounts for its low character. 'Heavenly Blue' is a ruthless aggressor not to be trusted in any cultivated spot, least of all in a rock garden where it will entrench itself as inextricably as a plague of wild onions. Reputable dealers are dropping 'Heavenly Blue' in favor of *M. armeniacum* but gardeners who gave the pest a foothold will not so easily be rid of it.

MUSCARI TUBERGENIANUM bears out L. H. Bailey's wryly humorous remark on muscari: "There are . . . several species with true blue flowers, the rarest color among flowers, though this would never be discovered in catalogues." Compared to the lavenders and violets hopefully advertised as sky blue, cerulean, or azure, *M. tubergenianum* is so purely blue that it seems to approach turquoise. By the chart it is a tint of cobalt with highlights of spectrum blue. In the garden, *M. tubergenianum* exactly matches a floret of *Brunnera macrophylla* (syn. *Anchusa myosotidiflora*), perhaps the most brilliant mid-blue perennial easily grown at sea level. A narrow rim of spanking white intensifies the muscari's blueness like a jet trail in a June sky. For a final fillip, the muscari is topped by a fly-away coronet of light blue, tubular, sterile flowers which keep the massive spike from looking dumpy.

Regrettably *Muscari tubergenianum* doesn't return my admiration. Its broad fleshy leaves seem more vulnerable to winter damage than the stringy foliage of commoner sorts. The loss of a major portion of its food factory prevents the formation of strong offsets, and so the plant inevitably dwindles. Though not a satisfactory garden plant for the North, *M. tubergenianum* is such a magnificent advance in the matter of blueness that I eagerly await its use in hybridizing.

NARCISSUS ASTURIENSIS is the most endearing of the truly miniature daffodils, absurdly tiny, a garden trumpet reduced to dollhouse size. Just as a chickadee is small for a bird but just the right size for chickadees, so *N. asturiensis* carries its 2½″ height with jaunty assurance, confident that nothing further could be asked in the line of daffodils. When paired with *Hyacinthus azureus*, another wrong-way-telescope version of a garden flower, the two might stand as principals in a Tom Thumb wedding.

By good fortune, *Narcissus asturiensis* is fairly easy to grow and keep—not foolproof by any means but increasing modestly when its needs are met. In my experience it does best under light shade and in richer and moister soil than you'd ordinarily give a daffodil. The pea-sized bulbs should be set about one and a half inches deep and completely surrounded by sand to insulate them from fungus-bearing humus particles, a standard precaution with all choice bulbs.

Narcissus asturiensis is still sometimes listed by its former name, *N. minimus*. According to H. W. Pugsley in his *Monograph of Narcissus, Subgenus Ajax*, the geographical name (from the mountains of the Asturias in northern Spain) has priority. While explaining the origin of the new name to visitors at the International Flower Show, I unexpectedly got confirmation of my belief that the little daffodil likes moisture. A listener exclaimed, "I studied in the Asturias one summer and it rained all the time!"

SCILLA BIFOLIA, like *Chionodoxa sardensis*, has the merit of earliness but little carrying power. Its small stars are a rather dull shade of slaty blue—or, less commonly, white or pinkish. The scapes are weak and apt to be knocked down in harsh weather. With its faults, *S. bifolia* has some distinctive charms, especially on close inspection. Departing from the scillas' usual chime of dangling bells, the flowers of *S. bifolia* stand out on stiff pedicels while their segments recurve like those of a turk's-cap lily, revealing a fluff of stamens. Since *bifolia* increases with moderation it can be used where *Scilla sibirica's* headlong seeding would prove a hazard.

SCILLA SIBIRICA, with *Muscari* 'Heavenly Blue,' must be among the most widely grown of midspring bulbs—and I use the word "widely" with double emphasis. Both jump the boundaries of the garden, spreading at the whim of wind and water through shrubberies and under hedges, invading lawns and escaping into the fields. While the gloomy grape hyacinth rates as a pest, the scilla's brilliant blue flood is welcome in all but the most select sites. One of its most delightful uses is as a carpet under early-flowering shrubs and trees. A weeping cherry trailing its delicate pink garlands over a pool of blue scillas is the joy of the neighborhood for its season and lives as a keen pleasure in the memory long after the flowers are spent.

SCILLA SIBIRICA 'SPRING BEAUTY' (syn. *S. s. atrocoerulea*) is the giant of its tribe. Since it is sterile, its multiple flower spikes last a long time in good condition. Even though 'Spring Beauty' presents no threat of invasion, it is not a plant for the rock garden. Its dominating size and the intensity of its Prussian blue flowers—a color so electrifying that it seems artificial—would overpower smaller companions and disrupt the harmony of a carefully scaled and balanced planting.

After seeing 'Spring Beauty' fairly shout down softer colors, I set it among some clumps of the reputed Welsh native *Narcissus obvallaris*, a chunky, strong yellow daffodil quite capable of holding its own against any competition. *N. obvallaris* stands from 10″ to 12″, too tall for a miniature yet undersized for a garden hybrid. Since 'Spring Beauty' is just a little shorter, the two are ideally suited. If grouped at the turn of a path or in a bay between shrubs, well away from bulbs of contrasting size, 'Spring Beauty' and *N. obvallaris* make a focal point of compelling attraction.

SCILLA SIBIRICA TAURICA is a refined edition of the type, subdued in manners and in color. It wears the same misty tint of cobalt blue as *Hyacinthus azureus,* stripes and all, with conspicuous dark blue anthers to add a bit of strength. Such a gentle and harmonious flower deserves to be widely known yet few dealers list it.

Unlike most bulbs, S. s. *taurica* doesn't bloom all at once but sends up a series of flower stalks at leisurely intervals. Because of its extended blooming period, *taurica* will sometimes be on hand to complement *kaufmanniana* tulips and intermediate daffodils such as the lovely N. *triandrus albus* and the hybrids 'Lintie' and 'Beryl.' I once had a stand of *taurica* at the edge of a woodland path where it was joined by some self-sown *Claytonia virginica.* The pink-veined spring beauties and blue-striped scillas made a delectable combination, quite unplanned but well worth repeating.

SCILLA TUBERGENIANA is a recent introduction from northern Persia and an invaluable asset in the early garden. Let me say at once that its color is too pale, so insipid that I dismissed it on first sight as inconsequential. Not at all put out of countenance by my disapproval, the scilla held its ground, increasing so prodigally that in a few years it formed a mound of flowers so broad that two hands could scarcely cover it.

The flowers of *Scilla tubergeniana* are similar to those of *Puschkinia scilloides,* being the faintest of watery blues with a slightly darker midrib. Resemblance ends there: in fact, the scilla's chief merit lies precisely in its difference.

Because of its tardy blooming, *Puschkinia scilloides* properly belongs in a later chapter. I mention it here only to point up the superiority of *Scilla tubergeniana.* Bluntly and briefly, the puschkinia is not a good garden subject. Its flowers are bunched at the end of an ungainly scape far above the scant

leaves. To make things worse, the stem goes limp in hot sun—
a hazard it inevitably suffers in mid-April—so that the sym-
metry of a patch is lost in a snaggle of drooping, snaky lines.

Scilla tubergeniana blooms at the beginning of March, so
eagerly that its flowers open in the cleft of the leaves while
still below ground level. The lengthening stem pulls more and
more flowers free until it reaches its full 5″ height. Even
though thickly set with large flowers, the scapes are stout
enough to hold erect in rainstorms or even to raise themselves
after being flattened by snow.

Though *Scilla tubergeniana* has little appreciable fragrance
—to a human nose, at least—it is madly attractive to honeybees. Working at fever pitch, they scramble over the flowers
and even force their way deep into the throat to search the
buds. Despite their activity, few capsules form, and these rot
off before seed can ripen so there is no problem of invasion.

Scilla tubergeniana is taller than most of the early miniatures but its flowers start at ground level—unlike *Puschkinia
scilloides*—and so relate closely to even the tiniest crocus.
Fluffy texture and uncompetitive color make S. *tubergeniana*
a flattering background for pastel crocuses as well as a harmonizer between conflicting shades.

Since it is the nature of gardeners never to be satisfied, I
could wish that *Scilla tubergeniana* had a stronger tinge of
blue in its blood, enough to make its presence more decisive
and perhaps enable it to register accurately on color film. By
the same token, I wish *Hyacinthus azureus* would flower several weeks earlier so that it could pair with the lovely yellow
crocus in the *chrysanthus* complex. Put them together and
you might get an earlier hyacinth, a bluer scilla. Both belong
to the lily family so a hybrid is not impossible. Chionoscillas
already exist. Why doesn't some adventurous experimenter try
for a hyascilla?

7

A Second Spring

If spring comes to the winter garden with the first crocus of January, it should logically end in late March when *Crocus vernus* 'Haarlem Gem' goes by. In the outside world, however, spring is little more than a rumor. Here and there in sheltered fence corners forsythia hangs out a few trial bells but it will be several weeks before star magnolias and Dutch crocus mark the arrival of spring in conventional gardens. We winter gardeners may as well enjoy a second spring while waiting for the rest of the world to catch up.

The transition between March and April is as boisterous as a tide rip. One day may be sultry at noon and rich with the delicious smell of wet earth steaming in the sun, while the next is lashed by chilling rain or snow flurries. A small group of plants seems particularly suited to this wayward season. A little too late to be classed as winter flowers, they yet have a fugitive air that sets them apart from the robust company of the conventional spring border. Anemones, the ethereal *Narcissus triandrus albus,* and low-growing species tulips would be swamped physically as well as visually by billows of candytuft or creeping phlox. These gentle flowers of the interim period need an uncrowded setting, and therefore belong in the disciplined confines of the rock garden.

ANEMONES have the disarming simplicity of midsummer daisies but with a fleeting air befitting their folk name of windflower. Those that disqualify themselves as reliable garden subjects by making leaf growth in the fall are discussed with other problem plants in the next chapter. Happily other species are prudent enough to stay below ground until the weather moderates in early April. Restrained in color as well as in behavior, these species flaunt no scarlets but confine themselves to a modest range of blue-violet, white, and subdued pink. Most are durable; a few seed freely enough to form lavish drifts.

Orthodox bulbs like those of tulips and daffodils are seemly containers for embryo flowers. Anemone rhizomes look like trash left on the compost screen: knotty sticks or swollen burls with no outward promise of the dainties they enclose. Tough and woody though they appear, the rhizomes are in fact critically sensitive to drying while out of the ground. For this reason it is essential to order from bulb specialists who thoroughly understand how and when to ship exceptional plants so that they arrive in viable condition.

The lush spring growth of anemones may wilt in hot sun. They should be given the same exposure as hellebores, that is, shade from distant trees or from a west wall which cuts off morning sun but not light from the sky. Ample water is needed during the blooming season. Once dormant, the roots can get along with available soil moisture.

The beautifully cut leaves of anemones disappear quickly after flowering is done. To mark their site against accidental digging, as well as to cover the void they leave, a few sprigs of creeping thyme should be carefully planted above the rhizomes. The thyme will soon close into a solid carpet and is vigorous enough to renew itself if the brief but dense shade of the anemone foliage should cause threadbare patches.

After the anemone leaves have died off, a mulch of leafmold or rotted manure will promote increase below ground and provide a fertile coverlet for self-sown seeds.

ANEMONE APENNINA flowers toward the end of
April, several weeks after the Greek windflower, *Anemone
blanda*. Its soft blue daisies have more slender rays and are
held on such tall stems that they lose relation to the foliage.
Anemone apennina has always been a shy flowerer with me.
On all accounts it falls behind A. *blanda* as a garden subject.

ANEMONE BLANDA ATROCOERULEA is a splendidly
showy plant, producing quantities of broad-rayed daisies set
compactly on a cushion of dark green leaves. The flowers have
two ranks of petal-like sepals, the upper row being slightly
shorter than the lower so that both show to full advantage.

The typical *Anemone blanda atrocoerulea* is rich lobelia
blue with a light yellow disk. Some individuals have a white
circle around the disk, varying from a hairline to a broad halo,
markings that probably indicate interbreeding with the pea-
cock-eyed A. *pavonina*. I slightly prefer the unmarked forms
as the contrast between blue and yellow is more telling with
no intervening white zone. However a little variety is welcome
in a large planting and I cherish any color forms that collectors or chance seeding may offer.

ANEMONE BLANDA 'BRIDESMAID' is a very large variety, not pure white as advertised (candytuft is pure white and
very glaring in the garden) but softened with a wash of ivory.
The buds and the reverse of the flower when closed in gray
weather are attractively flushed with violet or dark rose. Instead of a disk, the center of the flower is a raised boss like a
tiny pale green thimble surrounded by a fringe of yellow stamens. The flower is an excellent subject for close-up photog-
raphy which brings out the detail of the center and also the
crystalline texture of the rays.

Seedlings covered the space between 'Bridesmaid' and *atrocoerulea*: it was evident that 'Bridesmaid' had become a
bride. Unhappily I left the garden before the seedlings reached

flowering age and will always wonder which parent the children favored.

ANEMONE NEMOROSA is a familiar wildflower of the British Isles and northern Europe, a lover of cool woods and streamsides. It is a charming flower with many fine named varieties selected for size or depth of color. Even the richest blues or rose-pinks have a delicate air and need to be grown in great concentration to make an effect.

Though both my gardens had wooded areas, I could never induce *Anemone nemorosa* to settle down, let alone increase. The Manhasset hillside was sunny and sharply drained; the New Jersey woods very wet in spring but later sucked dry by the interlacing surface roots of large trees. Neither site could guarantee coolness and a steady supply of moisture during the long summer, and this I believe accounts for my failure.

Gardeners with suitably moist woods may treat themselves to a collection of all the color forms of *Anemone nemorosa*: soft blues and violets, pink and rose, all white or white flushed on the reverse with varied tints of the basic colors. I have also grown, but failed to keep, a double white form, A. *n. alba plena*, a darling miniature with a flat collar of round sepals and a mounded center as soft and full as a swansdown powder puff.

DAPHNE MEZEREUM is a small deciduous shrub, usually under three feet tall, with a vertical branching habit that gives it a pinched appearance. Though not much to look at, the daphne is remarkable for its powerful fragrance, as pervasive as the smell of spice cookies fresh from the oven, but underlaid with a heavy floral scent, an astonishing presence on the cold March air.

Daphne mezereum blooms naked, its florets set closely along the stems like those of redbud. Both share the same doleful tone of magenta, the daphne being a little closer to crimson, the redbud duller and more distressing. Both have far prettier white forms, as scarce as they are desirable.

Daphne mezereum was once difficult to keep because it was weakened by scale insects which encrusted the bark and multiplied beyond any available means of control. With the introduction of Malathion, this serious drawback has been eliminated. The daphne resents root disturbance and so should be bought in small sizes, preferably from a pot or can, and planted where it need never be moved. It wants a rather poor soil, well limed but free from manure or other rich fertilizer, and the shade of tall shrubs or high-branched trees.

Because of the daphne's narrow habit, it is better planted in groups than as an isolated specimen. Companion flowers should be chosen with care: chionodoxas' violet-blues would bring out the daphne's lurking purple, and clear or sharp colors would make it dingy. My little thicket of *Daphne mezereum* was underplanted with *Scilla sibirica taurica* whose soft, hazy blue went agreeably with the daphne's muted tone and perhaps even nudged it a little way from magenta toward the scilla's complement, red.

EPIMEDIUMS are among the finest plants for spring gardens, seen far less often than their attractions merit. The light yellow *E. versicolor sulphureum* is a tall and open grower, spreading by underground stolons and therefore too aggressive for the rock garden. The spring foliage of *E. rubrum* is highly decorative, the fresh green leaflets being bordered or almost entirely suffused with copper and terra-cotta tones. When the flowers open, their crimson backs are sharply discordant with the orange-browns of the foliage. This color clash, together with the plant's slightly leggy habit, rate it below the strict standards of the rock garden.

EPIMEDIUM YOUNGIANUM NIVEUM is the jewel of the family, one of the rare plants with which the most crotchety of critics could find no fault. It is a neat grower, spreading slowly into rounded, woody tuffets. With age, the center of the plant becomes hollow, a welcome signal to divide the clump and extend the plantation.

Unlike the majority of early spring-flowering plants, epimediums retain their foliage all summer and would indeed be evergreen in a milder climate. The plants make a handsome cover for dormant bulbs and serve as protection besides, for their thickly meshed roots keep squirrels from digging.

Every detail of *Epimedium niveum* is distinctive yet in harmony with the whole. The leaflets, slender but of firm substance, are held in precise groups of three by stiff, wire-thin stems. The foliage pattern combines delicacy with dash in a way that suggests a brush drawing of bamboo, though on a greatly reduced scale.

The white flowers stand just above the mounded foliage on shining brown, wiry, branching stems to form an airy spray. Though epimediums belong to the barberry family, individual flowers have a faint resemblance to snowdrops. However, as the epimedium's cup is trimmed on top by four flyaway spurs, the effect is rollicking rather than demure.

Epimedium niveum has an ironclad constitution and the simplest of cultural requirements. Though considered a woodland plant, it grows and flowers quite as well in full sun as in shade. It does, however, prefer woods soil—acid and rich in humus—and should be given an occasional watering in scorching weather. A generous dressing of screened leafmold in fall will keep up soil fertility. Even more important, the mulch will cover seedling snowdrops planted among the clumps, helping to secure the tiny bulbs from rodents and from being washed out by winter floods.

The only other attention the epimedium needs is to have its wiry leaf stems shorn close to the surface of the clump during the fall clean-up. If this tidying is overlooked, the dainty spring foliage will be obscured by a bristle of yellow straws, now impossible to cut except one by one, and so firmly attached that a tug on a stem will often bring away a crown of the plant with its spray of buds.

NARCISSUS species, especially the tiny ones, are far from easy to keep. A few intermediates, though too large to be classed as true miniatures, are nevertheless so distinct from the garden giants they precede that they deserve a place in the transitional garden. In this same category are some hybrids with one wild parent. These gain vigor from their mixed ancestry, though usually at the cost of increased size and often a stem out of proportion to the flower—too tall in many jonquil hybrids, too stubby in those from N. *asturiensis*. The *triandrus* hybrids, many from the gifted hand of the Cornish breeder, Alec Gray, are as appealing as their names—'April Tears,' 'Frosty Morn,' 'Rippling Waters'—but so late that they coincide with conventional daffodils and are therefore outside the scope of this study.

NARCISSUS 'BERYL' is the result of an improbable marriage between the clownish N. *cyclamineus* and a garden *poeticus*. The only evidences of *cyclamineus* blood are early flowering and backswept perianth segments. These are tinged with yellow on first opening but soon fade to a seemly *poeticus* white. Instead of a flat *poeticus* ruffle, 'Beryl' has a bowl-shaped cup, the added length serving to balance the backward thrust of the perianth. The cup is orange with a red rim which unfortunately burns quickly when exposed to sun. If the flowers are wanted for exhibition, they should be cut almost as soon as they open and stored in water in a refrigerator. Another defect is the long, weak scape, apt to go limp and drop the flowers on their faces on the hot days that sometimes blast buds in early April. I have a note to try growing 'Beryl' through a low shrub, with the idea of giving some support to the stems and at the same time shading the soil above the roots.

NARCISSUS 'FEBRUARY GOLD' is another child of *cyclamineus*, mated this time with a yellow trumpet and standing midway between its parents. The flower is a good rich yellow with a slightly belled trumpet strongly toothed at the brim. The perianth segments are narrow and pointed, with just a trace of backward curve. To give its namer the lie by one month only, 'February Gold' will sometimes flower before the end of March but more usually in the first week of April. It is a tall grower, a foot or over, and so out of scale for the average rock garden.

I grew 'February Gold' between shrubs lining a broad path leading into the woods, a transition between formal plantings and the wild garden, and therefore entirely appropriate for a half-and-half hybrid. Because its size and color are bold enough to carry, groups of 'February Gold' can furnish one of the earliest focal points to catch the eye at some distance from the house.

NARCISSUS OBVALLARIS is by name and legend a native of Wales, though many authorities now regard it as a garden escape of European origin. Certainly *obvallaris* shows scant resemblance to the accredited English native, *N. pseudonarcissus*. The Lent Lily of the poets may have beauty when seen by the meadowful, but it is a bedraggled thing on close inspection. With drooping neck and a lank perianth hanging in its eyes, it looks as if it had been caught hatless in a cloudburst.

Narcissus obvallaris, on the other hand, is turned out with military smartness. It is a square-shouldered flower of uniform deep yellow, with a flat perianth set at precisely the correct right angle to the trumpet. A stout, erect stem gives *obvallaris* a Guardsman's carriage. Usually about 10" tall, the relatively large flower with its widely flared, ruffled trumpet has a substantial air—not squat nor top-heavy, but solid.

Because of its compression, *Narcissus obvallaris* can hold its own beside *Scilla sibirica* 'Spring Beauty,' a vibrant electric blue that eclipses flowers of lesser impact. Scilla and narcissus make such a compelling group that they should be given a bandstand of their own—a bay of foreground shrubs or the base of a prominent rock—well out of the way of more modest flowers which might suffer by comparison with the emphatic pair.

NARCISSUS TRIANDRUS ALBUS is a meltingly lovely flower, frail-looking, feminine, as different from brassy-bold *N. obvallaris* as two daffodils could possibly be. As a fact, *triandrus albus* doesn't look like a daffodil at all but more like a cluster of milk-white fuchsias. Better still, picture the fuchsia's bell with its long clapper of pistil and stamens, crown it with the wings of a cyclamen, and you have some notion of the enchanting appeal of the flower.

When *N. triandrus albus* first opens, it is the palest of straw yellows, passing to near white as it ages. In the young flower, the perianth segments roll back from the bell in a shallow sweep, in profile like a saucer set on an overturned cup, a most gracious confluence of curving lines. With age, the segments reflex until their tips meet, with a wingy twist that heightens their resemblance to a cyclamen.

A scape may hold as many as four flowers but two or three are more usual. The larger number is gratifying evidence that the bulbs are doing well but the less crowded clusters have more grace. Like its cousin Amaryllid, *Galanthus elwesii*, *N. triandrus albus* is too lovely in outline to have its design lost in mere mass. These two bulbs, with *Epimedium youngianum niveum*, form one of the happiest associations of any season, being perfectly matched in scale, mood, and delicacy. The snowdrop blooms first, its white bells showing to advantage above the tea-colored young leaves of the epimedium; narcissus and epimedium flower together; and the epimedium holds the field with its decorative foliage long after the bulbs have gone to rest.

Narcissus triandrus albus is not a vigorous grower. It seldom increases but manages to maintain itself where it is happy, though the formula for pleasing the plant is by no means agreed on. Alec Gray among other authorities advises a dry situation, but in my experience the narcissus did better in loamy woods soil and light shade than in the sun-baked rock garden. It may be that what passes for a dry situation in rainy England would be cruelly parched in our summer droughts. At any rate I am inclined to follow Bowles's recommendation for planting the bulbs: "They ask for a gritty, well-drained soil round the bulbs and some good loam lower down for the roots to reach in the growing season."

English books speak of *N. triandrus albus* as a free seeder. I regret that it has never set seed with me so that I could increase my stock as I do with the slow-dividing *Galanthus elwesii*. As a result I never have had enough *triandrus albus* dancing in my woods, and even more sadly, never enough to cut, for the winged bells are delightful in the house with foliage of their attendant epimediums. My consolation is that the bulbs are fairly inexpensive, that is, about $1.25 a dozen, which means that someone can grow them successfully. If I must occasionally replenish my stock, I can do so without depleting a rare species.

TRITELEIA UNIFLORA VIOLACEA, to use the name still found in catalogues, is the vegetable counterpart of the nursery rhyme character who fell asleep upon the King's Highway, woke to find her petticoats cut to her knees, and cried, "Oh deary, deary me, this is surely none of I!" The hapless triteleia has been so shuttled about by taxonomists that it never knows, when it goes to bed in summer, what name it will waken to in spring. Milla and brodiaea were early names; then triteleia; and now, according to Synge and the RHS *Dic-*

tionary of Gardening, the proper term is *Ipheion uniflorum*, which sounds appropriate, whatever it means. Through its earlier name changes the plant retained at least a secure foothold in the lily family, but now it has been completely dispossessed and transferred to the *Amaryllidaceae*.

Change of climate and seasons alone might be enough to upset a native of Peru and the Argentine, but *Ipheion uniflorum* is one of the few subequatorial plants that not only thrives in the North but may seed itself to the point of becoming a nuisance. For this reason it is advisable to grow it in a spot where its exuberant increase won't overrun frailer plants. When grown in a mixed planting, faded blooms should be snipped off before seed can form.

Ipheion uniflorum starts to bloom in early April and sends up a long succession of buds, making a charming show for many weeks. Its star-shaped flowers usually have six points but vary from four to eight. The color is a fresh light violet with deeper midribs to strengthen the design, and a dark eye encircling conspicuous yellow stamens. Seen from the back, the coloring is even more striking: the underside of each segment bears a purple-brown stripe which broadens over the funnel-like base in a way that recalls the marking of an alpine gentian.

In addition to free seeding, *Ipheion uniflorum* has another vice that must be taken into account: when bruised, its foliage gives off a fearful stench of garlic. The long grassy leaves are almost prostrate and can spill quite a distance from their base. It is prudent to plant the bulbs a good twelve inches away from the margin of a path or grass border so that they are safely removed from assault by lawnmower or the tread of an unwary foot.

TULIP species make a timely appearance toward the end of March. Winter flowers have had their day: the eye craves fresh stimulation. With dazzling colors and impressive size, tulips salute the mood of a second spring with a bold statement of confidence.

Not all species tulips are suitable for the rock garden, their catalogue descriptions notwithstanding. Some of the huge reds —*T. fosteriana* and its varieties and hybrids, and the gigantic *T. eichleri excelsa*—are simply overpowering. Others like the appealing *T. clusiana,* called the Lady Tulip or even more aptly, Peppermint Stick, can't be reconciled to our climate and seldom last more than one year.

Recent interbreeding of *TT. kaufmanniana, greigii,* and *fosteriana* have produced some agreeable flowers and some unpleasantly inflated mongrels. On the credit side, *T. greigii* transmits the unique markings of its leaves, some mottled with purple or brown, others striped with chocolate like the lining of Jack-in-the-pulpit's hood. To my mind, however, tulips are not primarily foliage plants. I am not willing to trade good proportion and crisp texture for any amount of leaf painting.

The difficulty is that *T. kaufmanniana* has very long segments, while the huge *greigii* opens to a rather lax bowl with recurving brim. When combined, these characteristics tend to produce segments of gross size and lessened rigidity, quite incapable of supporting their own weight. Accordingly many of the hybrids droop in a flop-eared way. Before ordering hybrids, it would be wise to make careful notes at a flower show or botanic garden so that you will be sure of getting tulips and not basset hounds.

TULIPA BATALINII is a dainty flower of cool color and neat design. Its 6″ to 8″ stems are furnished with slender rippled leaves and crowned by a single flower of pure, pale mimosa yellow. Stamens are a shade deeper; the stigma is the milky green of pistachio ice cream. The segments broaden from the base in a swelling curve, then narrow to a point similar to the mucro or little hook that tips the perianth segments of some daffodils.

Though I dislike dwarf bearded irises in general, for reasons I will advance in a later chapter, I must make an exception in the case of 'Blue Frost' which might have been bred expressly to complement *T. batalinii.* Instead of the huddled squatness of most of its tribe, 'Blue Frost' is lightly poised on a slim 6″ stem, while its briskly flaring falls give it an air-borne look. The color is as clear and crystalline as its name, and a white beard enhances its icy effect.

TULIPA KAUFMANNIANA is such an ingratiating flower that it is difficult to understand why hybridists feel impelled to tamper with it. The outer surface is variously flushed or banded with rose. When the long ivory segments reflex, revealing the deep golden throat ringed with carmine, it is clear that the folk name Waterlily Tulip is an apt one. To further the illusion, surround the tulips with a massed planting of *Chionodoxa gigantea* so that the almost stemless "lilies" may float on a pool of blue.

Tulipa kaufmanniana has many color forms, some resembling the type but with more pronounced rose-red exterior and throat markings. Others range through yellow tones from cream to saffron, with or without red blazoning on the outer surface. The salmon pinks I have tried are less successful. 'Shakespeare' in particular has the colors laid on so streakily that it almost appears to be the victim of viral infection. My favorite variety is 'Scarlet Elegance,' a selection from *T. k. coccinea.* Four inches high and as much across when fully expanded, the flower is dazzling vermilion with a gold throat, a vibrant note of color to warm the heart in the last blustery days of March.

It was always my pleasure, as I passed the sunroom windows, to glance down on the rock garden for the heartening sight of snowdrops and crocuses in flower against the snowy landscape. When the burnished stars of 'Scarlet Elegance' expanded over the scarcely thawed earth, their piercing redness gave an actual jolt, a little shock of delight that never failed to strike a spark no matter how often I looked their way.

TULIPA TARDA, often catalogued as *T. dasystemon*, is one of the easiest tulips to grow. In the lean, dry soil of its preference, *tarda* increases into nosegays of starry flowers, closely bunched and sitting tight on their rosettes of prostrate, dark green leaves. Surprisingly, *tarda* even flourishes under city conditions, though the fallout of greasy soot and the fumes of automotive traffic must be a far cry from the clean air of its home in the mountains of Turkestan.

In the cold of early morning or on overcast days, the buds and closed flowers of *T. tarda* are almost invisible, being camouflaged with drab greenish brown outer coats. When the sun warms them, all at once the planting is alight with brilliantly white flowers centered with gold, five or six to each bulb, crowded back to back in charming profusion.

Knowing that nearly all tulips originate in mountainous regions of bitter winters and desert-dry summers, one can understand why many are unable to adapt to such radically unfavorable conditions as open, wet winters and humid summers. For this reason it is especially gratifying to see *T. tarda* accept our alien climate with grace, growing and increasing with the utmost freedom and generosity.

TULIPA URUMIENSIS is possibly a geographical variation of *T. tarda* from which it appears to differ only in color. Like *tarda*, *urumiensis* is inconspicuous when closed, as its dull reddish bronze back blends with the color of wet earth. When it opens it mirrors the sun: the interior is deep golden yellow with the reflective gloss of a buttercup.

Almost stemless on first opening, the flowers bunch together in an eye-catching way which sometimes causes them to be taken for an unfamiliar sort of crocus. During their long display the flowers edge up until they stand 5″ to 6″ tall. There is of course loss of compactness but the flowers end by looking somewhat more like the accepted notion of what a tulip should be.

While tulips commanded our attention, all over the garden aubrieta, arabis, and creeping phlox have been maturing their buds. A few warm days will bring the rockery to the full exuberance of spring bloom and close the book on the winter garden.

8

The Gambling Spirit

A banned book becomes an instant best seller. If I say that gambling with difficult plants is recommended for experienced gardeners only, every beginner will feel compelled to dive headlong. Take a flyer or two for fun and excitement, but please, in your first years of gardening, pick the majority of your plants from the easy lists. With a backlog of successes, you can then tackle chancy subjects without loss of confidence.

If response to freezing were the sole element involved in plant survival, it would be easy to work out precise ratings by use of a hardiness zone map. In actual experience the factors governing survival go far beyond thermometer readings.

Both my gardens were in Zone 7a with an average minimum temperature between 0° and 10°. According to these statistics, growing conditions should have been similar. In practice, the first flowers of spring came a month or six weeks earlier in Manhasset than in Tenafly.

The critical differences lay not in temperature but in altitude and in the clarity and movement of air. The Manhasset garden was on a hilltop where the air was scoured clean by salt breezes from the Sound. The sun could exert its full warming force with no barrier of smog to dim it. Because of the elevated site, killing frost came late while light frosts often flowed harmlessly away downhill.

In contrast, Tenafly lies in a hollow behind the Palisades. Since air currents from the Hudson River are walled off, humidity and soot gather in a persistent haze that veils the sun. Without full sun heat to promote thaws, cold spells last longer without a break. As a result the ground froze deeply. Bulb growth was halted; evergreens, especially camellias and skimmias, suffered leaf burn because their roots were unable to take up water to replace what they lost in transpiration. In summer, steaming days and muggy nights were damaging—often fatal—to alpine plants bred in the clean dry air of high altitudes.

I have gone into so much detail to impress the fact that temperature alone is not a gauge of hardiness. With other powerful variables at work, it's impossible to predict how plants will fare even in neighboring sections of the same zone. Borderline plants carry no guarantee but you can tip the odds in your favor by combining natural advantages with a selected microclimate. If you can offer higher altitude, freer circulation of air, cooler nights, less smog, or a milder climate, it's a good gamble that you can induce some of my failures to settle in.

ADONIS AMURENSIS is, with *Pulsatilla vulgaris* and the hellebores, one of the few nonbulbous herbaceous perennials to make a substantial show in the early garden. The two would make a stunning pair if only the adonis were easier to secure and to establish. I tried it first as a dormant root which failed to show in spring. A replacement sent as a growing plant contracted some lethal fungus in transit and died of it.

Adonis amurensis comes in single and double forms, and in shades of yellow and apricot. With its boldly toothed petal tips, the double yellow form looks somewhat like a giant dandelion. Instead of the dandelion's uniform color, however, the adonis is centered with an upstanding crown of emerald green petaloids. Its leaves are intricately slashed, very soft in texture, and densely clothed with silky, silver down. This velvety pile, while a delight to eye and finger, undoubtedly accounts for susceptibility to rot from dampness in shipping.

I hope that *Adonis amurensis* may become generally available and that the secret of shipping it will be solved. The imagined picture of its great yellow ray flowers set among the fur-coated purple cups of *Pulsatilla vulgaris* is so appealing that I am eager to see it realized.

AMARYLLIS BELLADONNA is typical of a class of plants which are intractable in the North not by reason of innate tenderness but because they send up foliage in the fall. The common grape hyacinth is a rare exception. Though it shares the habit of fall growth, its stringy leaves are tough enough to survive extreme cold and are able to extract a living even from smog-veiled winter sunshine. The foliage of the majority of bulbs, however, is so badly injured by frost, wind, and ice storms that it can't manufacture enough food to sustain the life of the bulb.

I planted *Amaryllis belladonna* in the warmest, most sheltered spot I had to offer, right against the wall in a southwest corner, but even so its long fleshy leaves were cut to the ground by mid-December. The plant lingered for years, each spring pushing up the pitiful scarred stubs of its leaves a little higher, but of course never building up enough strength to produce a flower. Since A. *belladonna* is fixed to its South African timetable, not even the most inventive gardener can hope to reconcile it to the rigors of a northern winter.

Even in mild England, Bowles recommended growing *Amaryllis belladonna* on the south side of a greenhouse so that it could benefit from the heated walls. Synge adds that the amaryllis flowers best after a really hot summer and for this reason does well in climates like those of California. Obviously I was trying the impossible: the amaryllis is suited only to regions that are virtually free of frost.

ANEMONE CORONARIA is a smoldering, sloe-eyed beauty flowering in late April and early May and thus properly

belonging to the period covered in the previous chapter. However since difficult plants are recommended for advanced gardeners only, I think it best to treat them together rather than
in chronological sequence of bloom.

Like *Amaryllis belladonna*, *Anemone coronaria* makes
leaves in autumn but these are so nearly hardy that I feel the
plant has a fair chance of success in a selected microclimate.
My pictures of the De Caen varieties—'His Excellency,' dazzling blood-scarlet; 'Mr. Fokker,' rich blue-violet; and 'The
Bride,' white—were taken in April and May of 1963 after the
most devastating winter in my gardening experience. On February 8, 1963, the temperature dropped to —6° and stayed below freezing for two cruel weeks, dipping to 9° on the
twenty-second before the cold relented. I had mistakenly
planted the anemones at the south wall where a light snow
had melted away, leaving the fragile-looking foliage wholly exposed to winds of gale force. If most of the anemones survived
this outrage and a few even managed to flower, I feel they have
a very good chance of coming through a more normal winter.

I should however reverse my prescription and give them a
site where snow is likely to linger. For example, a big hemlock
will preserve a snowbank in its shadow long after sun-warmed
areas on either side are bare. I believe that this natural insulation might provide just the extra break that *Anemone coronaria* needs to pull it through the winter. The flowers are
beautiful. It's well worth a gamble.

ANEMONE FULGENS is in Gerard's phrase "a most
gallant flower . . . of a perfect redde colour . . ." Reputedly a
natural hybrid between AA. *pavonina* and *hortensis* where
their ranges coincide in southern France and Italy, *fulgens*
shows considerable variation as it leans toward one or the
other parent. The usual sort resembles a slender-petaled vermilion daisy with small black center ringed in straw yellow.
In the same lot I have found superior specimens whose

rounded, overlapping segments may indicate a further admixture of A. *coronaria* blood. These fine flowers are blood scarlet, far more intense than in the daisylike forms, and made even deeper by a velvet surface. The weakening yellow ring is present but largely concealed by a beaded fringe of steel blue anthers around a conical black boss.

Unfortunately this splendid form is no hardier than the common one, for *Anemone fulgens* repeats the suicidal habit of making leaf growth in autumn. It will give one encouraging season of bloom, for newly planted tubers send up only a few leaves in their first fall. Though these are destroyed, the tubers have enough reserve strength to flower and to replace the slight foliage loss. Once established, however, the fall growth is profuse. When this is wiped out, the plant is doomed. It may rally its last force enough to lift a leaf or two in spring but this will be its final appearance.

Most early spring flowers collapse within hours of being brought into a heated room, but *Anemone fulgens* has the invaluable property of lasting for days in water. Because of its wonderfully bracing color, a saving antidote for the gray monotones of winter, I would recommend growing *fulgens* in a cold frame for the sake of cutting even if it can't be considered a durable garden ornament in the North.

I haven't given up, though. Synge's description of *Anemone fulgens* ends: "L. often appearing in the autumn," which surely implies that this is not the invariable rule. If there is actually a strain of *fulgens* that consistently delays leaf growth until spring, I mean to track it down.

CYCLAMEN serve to typify another order of difficult plants, a whole genus branded as unreliable because some of its species, offered without a note of caution by American dealers, are in fact not hardy at all. To be sure, the fat corms of cyclamen are intolerant of storage, turning to mush in heated holds or during long delays at plant quarantine centers. Nevertheless when a firm, plump corm is received and planted, and when it grows and flowers but dies in midwinter, it's fairly clear that innate tenderness and not mailbag fatigue is to blame.

The trouble is that American dealers order blindly from European bulb growers without ever bothering to check on hardiness in this climate. Synge clearly states that *CC. libanoticum, cilicicum,* and *repandum* are "tender in cold districts." If they are uncertain in mild English winters, what chance have they in our severe climate? Yet these touchy species are listed without qualification in American catalogues. The disappointed buyer will naturally conclude that cyclamen are impossibly difficult and will miss the joy of growing the reliable members of this engaging and highly individual race.

Even these relatively tough species are not to be stuck in the ground as heedlessly as you would a snowdrop or scilla. They have quite definite cultural needs—not whims but requirements, as you will find to your cost if you ignore them. The chief problem is the control of water. The plants should be well supplied when in growth but kept as dry as possible while dormant. The corms are critically sensitive to standing water yet the shallow roots must never be allowed to dry out. It's a tricky balance to keep the soil rich in humus yet open enough to drain readily. A raised position on a little mound or terrace in the rockery helps to shed surface water and at the same time provides a suitable stage for the display of these small treasures.

Most writers advise the use of crumbled mortar rubble below the corms to supply lime and improve aeration. If you haven't a ruined building to pick at, ground limestone will do.

Cyclamen, especially the August-flowering *C. europeum,* are apt to wilt in the full blast of midday sun. An ideal position is to the northeast of tall trees, well out from the drip of branches, open to the sky, yet lying in the trees' shadow during the hottest hours of the day.

The next consideration, and an essential one, is to plant the corm right side up. This takes a bit of study: some species root from the top only, some from the bottom, and some every which way. Individual peculiarities will be described under each species. The rooting pattern is such a clinching means of identification that I wish Synge's plates had included corms and roots as an aid to visual memory.

Finally, plant the corms shallowly, not more than an inch or two below the surface; give them a dressing of finely screened leafmold and bonemeal in July while they are still dormant; and leave them alone forever. Cyclamen corms never divide but merely sit tight, growing fatter and more flowery with the years. The only method of increase is by seed. This is produced generously and safeguarded over winter by an ingenious device. As Parkinson describes it, "After the flowers are past, the head or seede vessell shrinketh downe, winding his footestalke, and coyling it selfe like a cable, which when it toucheth the ground, there abideth hid among the leaves, till it be grown great and ripe . . ." In spring the buried capsule, enormously inflated, swells to the surface. At the same time, its spiral tether rots off, freeing the capsule so it can float off on melting snow to start a new colony. In the garden, the capsule should be gathered before it opens, or ants will make off with the seeds in a night.

CYCLAMEN CILICICUM is the luckless charmer that first raised suspicion of the hardiness of cyclamen offered by American dealers. The corms arrived in top condition, firm and unblemished, and bloomed enchantingly in late October. The flowers, soft pink with a rose-red flare at the base, stood above round leaves with frosty tracings. Each plant could have been covered by a silver dollar but small as they were, their leaves were crisp and erect, their flowers profuse. Obviously *C. cilicicum* had established itself without shock and showed every sign of health and permanence. It was a sharp disappointment when the thriving plants shriveled and died in a snowless period of bitter cold.

Even though *Cyclamen cilicicum* is not hardy in the North, it is such an enchanting miniature that it should surely grace rock gardens in milder climates. For the guidance of those who can give it a good home, *cilicicum* roots from the middle of the underside. If you look carefully, you can make out tiny hard knobs on top from which the flowers develop. With any luck, traces of roots will remain on the corm to help you tell top from bottom.

CYCLAMEN EUROPEUM and CYCLAMEN NEAPOLI-TANUM form one of the most congenial associations in the garden, each one supplying virtues to cover the other's deficiencies. Since they dovetail so closely they will be treated as a pair.

Cyclamen europeum is found in central and southern Europe. From a geographical standpoint it would be expected to prove hardier than the more southerly *C. neapolitanum* but the reverse is true. In my experience and that of many authorities, *europeum* merely maintains itself where *neapolitanum* flourishes. In this case gardeners have the luck of the draw for *neapolitanum* is unarguably the handsomer plant.

Cyclamen europeum is not strictly an autumnal subject as it starts to bloom in late July but often continues well into September. Its flowers are a bit dumpy, with segments too short for their breadth, and of a rather dull shade of magenta. Lack of grace is redeemed by the gift of fragrance, a cool, springlike odor suggesting the scent of water lilies but lighter and more elusive.

The leaves of *Cyclamen europeum* contribute more to the partnership than do its flowers. The typical shape is a rounded heart with smooth margins but occasionally more pointed forms occur. The color is dark ivy green with scattered markings of a lighter grayed tone like carnation foliage. The leaves are less noted for beauty than for timeliness: they appear in midsummer and are in strong growth in late August when the first naked flowers of *C. neapolitanum* rise from the soil.

The leaves of *Cyclamen neapolitanum* are incomparably decorative but very slow to develop, not reaching their full potential until near the end of the flowering season. For ten months of the year thereafter they make an extraordinarily beautiful display. The leaves are bright spinach green and infinitely variable: some pointed like an arrowhead, some more nearly heart-shaped, others deeply lobed like an ivy leaf. The edges may be smooth, indented, or undulating, while the areas between the veins sometimes puff up in a quilted effect. All are lavishly frosted with traceries of silver and celadon green.

The flowers of *Cyclamen neapolitanum* are larger than those of *europeum*, admirably porportioned, and auricled, that is, furnished with a thickened white ring on the margins of the segments where they recurve from the brim. Seen from beneath with a hand lens, the base of the flower suggests a string of five white spools tied in a pentagon, each spool unwinding a carmine ribbon against the pale rose-pink petal. The presence of auricles may seem a trivial detail but it adds immeasurably to the grace of the flower, as it causes the segments to roll smoothly around the spool, curving inward before they expand above it. In contrast, the segments of *europeum* fold abruptly back on themselves, creased in a hard line that emphasizes their stubby appearance.

Cyclamen neapolitanum's long segments have the broadly curving outline of a paddle blade, with a half twist above the base that gives an effect of airy animation. The flowers hover like butterflies on 5" stems but expose a great deal of bare earth, not at all improved by their emerging buds and leaf stems which look like a tangle of pinkish-brown earthworms. When interplanted with *europeum*, their leggy look is diminished. No longer disembodied but firmly related to the plant world, they float with assurance above a foundation of borrowed foliage.

Both CC. *europeum* and *neapolitanum* produce albino forms, scarcer than the colored types and predictably more expensive. The white *neapolitanum* is ethereally lovely but less vigorous than the type, unhappily the case with most albinos since their loss of color results from genic deficiency. The frailty of *C. neapolitanum album* shows up in scantier bloom and greatly reduced seed formation. Nevertheless it is eminently worth growing by those who feel a protective tenderness toward fragile beauties. I have never found *europeum album* offered for sale but since the type is only a moderately good grower, it's a fair guess that the weaker white form would be unlikely to succeed.

Cyclamen europeum roots all over its large corm. Usually enough roots adhere to enable a gardener to note their direction and plant them pointing down. The corm of *neapolitanum* is a flattened disk, slightly hollow on top, rounded and featureless below like an inverted mushroom cap. Where the mushroom stem would be, the corm should show the knobby traces of flower stems and possibly some roots which proceed from the top only. For this reason *neapolitanum* should be planted a little deeper than the others, that is, two inches below the surface. Because of its shallow rooting, a yearly mulch of leafmold and bonemeal is essential for nourishment.

Cyclamen europeum may stand low on the scale of beauty but it tops all other varieties by reason of its magic properties. According to Gerard's direction, "Being beaten and made into troschies, or little flat cakes, it is reported to be a good amorous medicine to make one in love if it be inwardly taken." The more sophisticated Parkinson has his doubts—"But for any amorous effects, I hold it meere fabulous"—but I wouldn't let his skepticism spoil the sport.

Gerard's prescription holds an intriguing ambiguity. I had

Crocus chrysanthus 'Moonlight'
flowering in March in the open garden.

The fluffy, pale blue spikes of *Scilla tubergeniana*
make a harmonious foil for early crocuses.

Tulipa kaufmanniana 'Scarlet Elegance'
opens its burnished stars
before the end of March.

Crocus chrysanthus 'E. A. Bowles' and *C. tomasinianus* 'Whitewell Purple'
are outstanding individuals and delectable companions.

The flowers of *Pulsatilla vulgaris* are appropriately fur-coated
for chilly April. Mature foliage is so massive that the plant
is suitable only for large gardens.

Aubrieta deltoidea is spectacular in April bloom
and an excellent bulb cover for all seasons.

The soft blue-violet of *Chionodoxa gigantea*
is appealing in sun or shade and especially effective
as an under-planting for *Tulipa kaufmanniana*.

Epimedium youngianum niveum is valuable for April bloom
and for decorative foliage throughout the season.
Its matted clumps protect bulbs from rodents.

8

supposed that love potions are given to the reluctant fair one, but since it would be difficult to administer even a small troschy without being detected, it appears that cyclamen may be a charm to put would-be gallants in the mood for courting. I submit the inquiry as a project for some lively herb society and would be much interested in following the progress of investigation.

CYCLAMEN ORBICULATUM is the catchall name under which the winter-flowering *CC. atkinsii, coum,* and *hiemale* are currently lumped. My acquaintance—unhappily too brief to be conclusive—is limited to the variety which came to me as *C. atkinsii roseum.*

The buds developed in midwinter, lying flat on the ground presumably to take advantage of any snow cover. They were erect and ready to open when I left the Tenafly garden on January 26. After the movers had loaded and gone, I leaned my forehead against the window for a last look at the flowers I had cared for: the bright crocus, snowdrops, and the carmine buds of *Cyclamen orbiculatum* which I was not to see flower. Of all the goodbyes I had to say, this held the keenest pain.

HELLEBORES are as valuable for their boldly designed evergreen leaves as for their flowers, some of which are beautiful and some decidedly queer. In a garden of bulbs, here today and underground tomorrow, the presence of a solid, almost sculptural feature is eminently worth cultivating.

Hellebores are deep-rooting, greedy plants. Since they resent disturbance, their site should be deeply dug and enriched with enough humus, lime, and bonemeal to last their life span. Manure is considered risky in direct contact with roots but makes a beneficial mulch for established plants.

Shade from deciduous trees will keep the succulent flower stalks from wilting in midday heat. A wall facing west or somewhat north of west serves the purpose equally well by shielding the plants from all but the temperate afternoon sun. Shelter from cutting ground winds—a dense hedge, fence, wall, or mound—is desirable to protect the handsome foliage from being bruised and tattered in snowless winters.

The last requirement, a need for pure air, is at once the most essential and the most difficult to provide. Parkinson was fully aware of the damaging effect of tainted air on sensitive plants. Though he wrote of *Anemone coronaria*, his warning applies as aptly to hellebores: the plants will grow "if the place where you sowe them, be not annoyed with the smoake of Brewers, Dyers, or Maultkils, which if it be, then will they never thrive well." Plants that languished in the small smoke of an Elizabethan brewery can hardly be expected to endure the massive air pollution of today's cities and industrial complexes. As proof of Parkinson's observation, *HH. foetidus, orientalis,* and *niger* throve well in Manhasset's clean, salt-washed air, but only *H. orientalis* survived the heavy atmosphere of New Jersey.

HELLEBORUS CORSICUS is a most distinguished plant, one with an air of quality. The polished, rich green leaves, typically three-lobed, are held on short petioles to form a low mound. To my great regret, *H. corsicus* falls short of being reliably hardy in Zone 7a. I had admired a luxuriant border of *corsicus* in Carl Starker's garden in Jennings Lodge, just south of Portland, Oregon. Because of the exceptional beauty of its foliage, I tried it several times in different situations. No matter what exposure I gave the plants, they were weakened by winter damage and lasted at most for three years. They never flowered with me but gardeners in milder climates may expect great heads of yellow-green flowers shaped like shallow bowls.

HELLEBORUS FOETIDUS is an English native, a more forthright plant than *H. corsicus*, perhaps a trifle unkempt and best suited to rough places such as the edge of shrubbery. The leaves are slashed into narrow fingers, usually nine in number, spreading far apart and drooping at the wrist. The open design of a few leaves suggests the economy of a Chinese brush drawing, but in a mass the confusion of lines gives a restless effect.

Buds appear close to the ground in February and gradually ascend to a height of 24". In early March the straggly, irregular inflorescence dangles a quantity of bell-shaped flowers, light green with a rim of burnt orange, an odd but agreeable color scheme. Flyaway bracts jutting up among the flowers add to the plant's slightly disordered air. As I say, *Helleborus foetidus* is not a neatly groomed plant yet it has a sort of rakish appeal that fits it for an informal setting.

Don't let the folk name Stinking Hellebore put you off. The plant is odorless unless bruised, and even then the smell isn't markedly offensive.

HELLEBORUS NIGER is the Christmas Rose of tender legend, a buttercup in sober fact, a treasure by any standard. Parkinson lovingly described "the true and right kinde, whose flowers have the most beautiful aspect, and the time of his flowring most rare, that is, in the deepe of Winter about Christmas, when no other can bee seene upon the ground . . ."

In the North *Helleborus niger* seldom blooms before March and extends into April, thus overlapping the *H. orientalis* hybrids known as Lenten Roses. Its leaves are dull green, in no way competing for attention with the glistening white flowers they guard. The flowers have an unearthly beauty, a matchless purity enhanced by a prominent fluff of yellow stamens. Some individuals are faintly tinted with pink or apple green, variations that add interest without altering the overall impression of crystalline whiteness.

When the flowers have been pollinated, the stamens fall off, their place being taken by protruding carpels. The aging flower passes from white to pale green and then to a soft pink-ish tan, remaining intact for a period of weeks, sometimes until the seeds are ripe and ready to harvest.

As befits a reigning beauty, *Helleborus niger* is a handful of temperament. *Curtis's Botanical Magazine* for 1787 says of it, "Like most other alpine plants, it loves a pure air, a situation moderately moist, and a soil unmanured . . . neither this species nor the *hyemalis* [*Eranthis hyemalis*, then classed as a hellebore] thrive very near London." If *H. niger* found the air of eighteenth-century London too corrupt for its health, it can hardly be expected to flourish in today's city atmosphere, fouled with the fumes of automotive traffic, incinerators, and power plants.

In addition to its demand for clean air, *Helleborus niger* is intolerant of disturbance and as a result is difficult to ship or even to transplant in one's own garden. Small plants from pots can be shifted without disrupting the root system but bare root plants—especially imported ones which have suffered the further ordeal of fumigation—have a minimal chance of surviving.

The best way to establish a colony is to sow fresh seed where the plants are to grow. This takes a fair stock of patience. According to my records, seed gathered in my handkerchief on June 1, 1954, and sown within the hour produced its first blooms in April 1957. I had previously bought a few plants which suffered the expected setback, including the loss of some to a blackening fungus disease. The seedlings, growing without check, soon overtook and eventually surpassed the older plants in size and vigor. If you haven't access to fresh seed, this may be the best way of getting a start: buy plants with the hope of harvesting seed from them, and then keep lively youngsters coming along to replace the elders that succumb to shock.

As a cut flower, *Helleborus niger* is as lasting as it is ravishingly beautiful. (Arrange the flowers, please, with pachysandra

leaves and not their own precious foliage.) If you want to ornament the house as well as the garden, you will need so many
plants that building up a stock by seed is a necessary economy.
When your seedlings open their first flowers, you'll think the
three-year wait well spent.

HELLEBORUS ORIENTALIS, or the hybrids sold under
that name, appear in this chapter solely on the basis of blood
relationship and not by reason of difficulty. Aside from an ex-
cusable objection to dry soil and baking sun, the plants are utterly accommodating, seeding themselves with abandon and
submitting with good grace to being transplanted even in
full bloom.

The pure strain of *Helleborus orientalis* has creamy flowers,
while its hybrids with *HH. purpurascens, atrorubens,* and a
legion of other species show their mixed blood in a wide range
of colors. My favorites are the pure whites, the cool pale
greens, and those with infusions of shell pink in various intensities. I can accept a few sullied straw whites for the sake
of their dull crimson freckles, but those veined with maroon
look uncomfortably like bloodshot eyes, while the denser pur-
ple-maroons resemble raw liver. Since the *orientalis* hybrids
come so readily from seed and flower in their second year,
plants that fail to please can be tossed out as lightly as you
would discard off-color petunias.

Helleborus orientalis hybrids can be used to good account
wherever a mass of heavy-textured, evergreen foliage is called
for. Since my New Jersey rockery was placed by necessity
against the house walls, *H. orientalis* helped screen the ugly
concrete footing of the western face, though it couldn't take
the full blast of sun against the south wall. I also used *orientalis* extensively and with good effect in the woodland garden
where it made a transition between tall background shrubs
and the smaller plants—tiarella, epimedium, asarum—that
bordered the paths.

IRISES are thought of as indestructible plants. Holding their own among weeds, they mark the sites of forgotten farmhouses as staunchly as lilacs. Outdated varieties are hard to dispose of. Tossed on the compost heap or over the hedge, they'll contrive to sink roots and flower again.

To gardeners who have seen bearded and Siberian irises thrive on neglect, the difficulty of keeping bulbous irises will come as a jolt. Hardiness is not a factor: the plants are inured to severe cold in their native mountains in Asia Minor, the Caucasus, and Turkestan. The rub is that these mountains are totally arid in summer, sometimes baked dry for months without a break. In this country, a foot of rain may fall in the same interval. When softened by constant moisture, irises of the *reticulata* section are subject to Ink Disease, *Mystrosporium adustum*. This fungus first forms black patches on the netted outer tunic and then, if not checked, penetrates and destroys the bulb.

There are three ways to handle bulbous irises. The best, if you have the facilities, is to grow them in pots in an alpine house where the lovely blooms are sheltered from sleet and splattering mud. As an added advantage, irises in pots can be moved after flowering to a cold frame to complete their growth cycle out of the public eye. Bulbous irises have stringy leaves that may top 18″ before they dry off. Since these are brittle and easily broken by wind, it is a point of protection as well as of neatness to keep the plants under cover during their straggly period. Once dormant, the bulbs should be stored in a dry, warm place until autumn.

The second method of handling bulbous irises is the one outlined by W. R. Dykes in his great monograph, *The Genus Iris*. He advises lifting the bulbs at least every other year as soon as the leaves have died completely away. Badly diseased bulbs are burned; the rest are soaked for two hours in a bath of 1 part formalin to 300 parts water. After disinfection the bulbs should be dried in the shade and stored in dry sand until planting time in September.

If bulbous irises are grown in a bed by themselves, digging may not be objectionable, but I am concerned with the appearance of a diversified, year-round garden. To get at bulbs it would be necessary to tear up the mat-forming plants that cover them. In a thickly planted garden, even with the guidance of a chart, bulbs would be dug at the risk of slicing close neighbors.

The third method, then, is to plant the bulbs in a pocket of sand on a slope or plateau and let them take their chances. I have treated the relatively inexpensive *reticulata* varieties in this manner, electing to replace them when necessary rather than disrupt established carpeting plants by digging the bulbs.

Choicer varieties such as the *reticulata-histrioides major* hybrids are higher in price and therefore planted in such small numbers that lifting them is not a major excavation. To make sure that no offsets are lost, I suggest making 4"-deep trays of ¼"-wire mesh—the stiff galvanized screening called hardware cloth—and sinking them in gritty, limed, humus-enriched soil. Spread an inch of clean coarse sand over the bottom of the tray, set the bulbs on it four inches apart, and cover them completely with more sand. This insulates bulbs against contact with fungus-bearing humus particles. The tray should then be filled with prepared soil, mounded slightly above the surrounding grade for maximum drainage.

As companion plants, I would choose those that throw out trailing stems without rooting: the silvery *Artemisia schmidtiana nana*, *Geranium sanguineum lancastriense*, or a dwarf form of *Campanula carpatica*. Since these plants die back to the base over winter, their early spring growth doesn't compete with the flowering of the iris. In summer when the iris basket needs to be lifted, the trailing skirts of the plants can be draped over the spot to hide the raw earth.

Irises of the *reticulata* section have individual modifications that set them apart from the more familiar bearded sorts. The flowers in profile are funnel-shaped: the falls, contradicting their name, rise at angles around 45° from the horizon, with only their tips turning downward. Instead of the broad arches of bearded iris, the standards of the *reticulatas* are reduced to narrow ribbons or even to mere bristles. When these stand erect or point slightly outward, they expose the hollow of the funnel with a rather meager effect. *Iris reticulata* in particular is so pared down that it seems as if its designer had skimped in material. The better species have greatly elaborated style branches, expanded, pinked or ruffled, and recurved like drake tails. As their tips curl up and inward, these petal-like structures fill the central void and to a great extent compensate for the sparseness of the standards.

The leaves of the *reticulata* group are as singular as their flowers. On first appearance they look like a bundle of white skewers, for each leaf is furnished with a horny tip to pierce frozen ground. Mature leaves are grassy but can be distinguished by their grayish color and—with one exception—four prominent ribs. These are spaced irregularly so that a section is not rectangular but kite-shaped, that is, like a high-waisted diamond with concave sides.

IRIS BAKERIANA is the exception: its leaves are cylindrical with eight lengthwise grooves so evenly ranked that a sketch of a cross section could double for a cogwheel. Under a hand lens, the flower reveals an intricately detailed color pattern. The pointed tip of the fall is blackish violet with the velvet richness of a pansy petal. The central area appears bright blue but under magnification shows an oyster white ground heavily powdered with deep violet dots and broken lines. Standards are chicory blue and lightly curled so that they close over the central cavity.

Against the south wall *Iris bakeriana* flowered in mid-February, the bitterest stretch of a northern winter. The flowers were surprisingly durable but the leaves—each bulb had only two—were battered to death by wind and snow. It may be that a colder exposure would delay flowering. Someone else can try the experiment. As for myself, I am too fond of the valiant little iris to subject it to another winter in the open. With only two leaves for security, the margin for survival is too slight to make *Iris bakeriana* a good gamble.

IRIS DANFORDIAE is another eccentric, following the family norm of four-sided leaves but differing sharply in form and color. Its standards have shrunk to tiny spurs, almost invisible to the naked eye. To some extent the standards are replaced by greatly enlarged style branches. As these fail to reach the height of the missing standards, the flower is somewhat squat in outline.

Odd as its construction may be, the color of *Iris danfordiae* is an even more dramatic departure from the family livery. The style branches are sulfur yellow shading to citron, with a bar of emerald green on either side of the ridge. The falls are slightly deeper, nearing canary yellow, with a raised orange bee guide along the center line. The flower gets its punch from a peppering of olive-green and bronze spots, thickly concentrated on the haft and shoulder of the falls and thinning out over the blade.

The difficulty with *Iris danfordiae* is that it splits up into quantities of tiny pips which may take three or four years to reach flowering size. The wire basket device wouldn't work in this case as the pips would sift through the bottom. Pots are indicated but these are a hazard when sunk in the ground over winter because they absorb moisture. When this turns to ice, it may seal the drainage hole and let the pots fill with water from surface thaws. Since I can think of no way of converting *I. danfordiae* to the role of permanent garden display, I reluctantly consign it to pots in an alpine house.

IRIS HISTRIOIDES MAJOR is a superlative flower, perhaps the most fantastically beautiful ornament of the winter garden and quite surely the most improbable. The bud rises naked from the earth, looking unpromisingly like a giant thumb blue-gray with cold. As many times as I've seen it, I still feel a tingle of unbelief when the flower spreads its blue wings like a tropical butterfly in the frosty air.

In Manhasset's undiluted sunshine *Iris histrioides major* flowered as early as the third week of February. It came later in New Jersey but always opened in time for the International Flower Show in early March. Visitors coming in from snowy suburbs could, after some persuasion, believe that crocuses and snowdrops had really been gathered that morning from an outdoor garden. The regal iris was regarded with marked skepticism even by informed plantsmen. Astonishing enough indoors, the iris is an unearthly apparition in the scarcely thawed garden.

Unlike the skeletal *Iris reticulata, I. histrioides major* is cut with a generous hand. Heavy substance and nearly horizontal falls give it a sturdy, square-shouldered look. The falls are blue-violet with a velvet finish. A small central area of white is almost covered by an imprint of black-violet bars and chevrons, with a raised bee guide of deep yellow. Standards and expanded style branches are lobelia blue, a little lighter in tone and texture than the falls but close enough for unity. The standards are spoon-shaped while the style branches, nearly as large and feathered at the tips, spring upward in a jaunty way.

To add to its attractions, *Iris histrioides major* has an engaging way of carrying itself a little on a slant. Depending on their direction, a pair may seem to exchange the poised bow and curtsy of a minuet. If several cock their heads together, they suggest listeners absorbed in conversation.

For the record *Iris histrioides major* has survived a drop to

24° without injury. Since it has happily been spared worse insult, I can't say what its threshold of tolerance might be. While the flower is remarkably resistant to cold, it may suffer mechanical damage when its broad falls are dragged down by the weight of snow. When a storm is forecast, it's a wise precaution to cover the planting with overturned bushel baskets, topped by three or four bricks in case of high wind.

I feel that *Iris histrioides major's* exceptional beauty justifies any care needed to preserve and increase one's stock. The bother of planting in wire baskets and lifting annually is not too great a price for such magnificence.

One of the interesting new developments in the field of small bulbs has been the introduction of hybrids between *Iris histrioides major* and *I. reticulata*. These combine the broad proportions of the former with the latter's staying power. Since an increasing number are offered each year, it appears that these hybrids are meeting the enthusiastic reception they deserve.

IRIS 'HARMONY' was the first *histrioides* x *reticulata* I grew. It proved a splendid grower, increasing satisfactorily. In appearance it stands midway between its parents. Leaves are present but stay well below the level of the flower. The falls rise slightly, with tips carried horizontally for a clear display of their markings. The color is midnight blue with very little difference between standards and falls. Because of its intense color, 'Harmony' is very effective when contrasted with pale yellow crocuses such as *C. chrysanthus* 'Moonlight.'

IRIS 'JOYCE' is a newcomer and an immediate favorite. It is flax blue with dashes of cornflower blue on its white-centered falls. The light color suggests that the *reticulata* 'Cantab' may have been one parent, with the blood of *histrioides major* giving greater breadth and substance. 'Joyce' is not quite so well proportioned as *histrioides major*: a very short tube sets it too close to the ground, and its standards fall away from the center, almost repeating the angle of the falls. It is however desirable for its delightful color. As for its form, I'm confident that other and finer hybrids are in the making.

In its trial year 'Joyce' produced two flowers from each bulb, a very promising sign of vigor. I can't report on its staying power as I left the garden before a second spring.

As a precaution with 'Joyce' and all other untested hybrids, I suggest two equal plantings: one to be left in its sand pocket, the other set in a wire basket for annual lifting and drying. A count of flowers in succeeding years will show whether the irises take after their *histrioides major* or *reticulata* parent, and need intensive care or intelligent neglect.

IRIS RETICULATA has been described indirectly by comparison with its opposite. Its bad points are a mosquito-thin outline and the tall leaves that obscure the flowers in a grassy thicket. On the credit side, the *reticulatas* have a wider range of color since neither *histrioides major* nor its hybrids can so far boast red-purple tones. In general the *reticulata* varieties have more conspicuous bee guides, deeping from orange almost to scarlet. Best of all, they will persist for years if their situation is chosen for optimum drainage and sun baking.

The type to some extent makes up for the slenderness of its segments by the richness of its color. The falls are spectrum violet with a small white area and prominent orange ridge while the style branches add an accent of reddish amethyst.

Many people exclaim with delight at the violet fragrance of *Iris reticulata*. Others—I regret to be among them—detect only a fresh, flowery, but quite indeterminate scent.

IRIS 'CANTAB' is smaller than the type and even more enmeshed in foliage but it was a prime favorite before the more spectacular 'Joyce' nosed it out of first place. 'Cantab' is the most enduring of bulbous iris I've grown, increasing to form telling clumps of dainty flowers and making up in profusion what it lacks in size. It is a hazier blue than 'Joyce,' bluebird blue by the chart, with standards paler and muted, a subdued scheme enlivened by a bee guide of brilliant orange.

IRIS 'J. S. DIJT' has more breadth than the average *reticulata*, with enlarged style branches that stand nearly as tall as the standards. The color is saturated red-purple—doge purple by the chart, an unfamiliar term that nevertheless conveys a sense of richness. The white area, usually centered on the fall, is confined to the haft. In its place the pigment of the falls seems to be concentrated to its fullest intensity, making a rich field for the gold bee guide. This is rounded, not merely ridged, and, being spotted with purple along its sides, looks like a plump velvet caterpillar.

'J. S. Dijt' is larger and later than 'Cantab' but the colors are so delectably mated that the two should be planted together in the hope that a part of their flowering times may coincide.

IRIS UNGUICULARIS was cited in Chapter 2 as an example of a hardy plant with flowers too tender to survive in the North.

LYCORIS RADIATA was the sensation of the garden when it first bloomed in mid-September. Its wheel-like umbel carried a miniature turk's-cap lily at the end of each spoke—not harsh orange but a lovely soft tone of jasper red with a rosy flush. The recurved segments, charmingly rippled along their margins, were balanced by the thrust of protruding pistil and stamens.

My delight in the discovery of a new flower was short-lived. My note for October 5 reads "Unhappily, lycoris shows leaf growth—soft, pale, tender-looking." As in the case of *Amaryllis belladonna*, the lycoris foliage was wiped out by cold.

Though the leaves made a feeble appearance for a year or two longer, the bulbs never gathered strength enough to flower again, and finally died away. This is a plant for mild climates where frosts are infrequent and not prolonged. My bulbs were a gift from Mrs. George Heath of the Daffodil Mart in Virginia so the lycoris is assuredly hardy from Zone 8a south.

NARCISSUS species and their hybrids include some of the most seductive miniatures for the early garden. They display every charm of daintiness, precise design, and perfect balance—everything, in short, except ease of culture. In repeated trials some barely maintain themselves, some go all to leaf after their first year, and others—the tiny jonquils in sad particular—flower enchantingly once and then disappear forever.

The majority of miniature daffodils come from the mountains of Spain and Portugal where tender species would have been eliminated. Certainly the bulbs breeze through their first winter in the New York area so their hardiness can't be in question. Some factor of our summers—rain, temperature, humidity, low altitude—must differ radically from growing conditions in the daffodils' alpine habitat, with the result that bulbs fail to ripen and simply rot in the ground.

Alec Gray, the Cornish authority and breeder whose name is synonymous with miniature daffodils, recommends shallow planting: ". . . I should say as a general rule that they should go down rather more than twice their own height, in other words, a bulb, say ½ inch high, should have nearly an inch of soil on top of it when the earth has settled."

I know that I lean toward deep planting, having been plagued by squirrels in both gardens, and accordingly blamed my early losses on this tendency. In later tries of the bewitching little jonquils I distrusted my eye and checked the depth of the bulbs with a ruler. As a further test some were planted in open ground for the sun to bake. Others were set under mats of dwarf thyme in the hope that a net of wiry stems would make hard digging for squirrels and also that the roots of the thyme would quickly dry the ground after rain. Unqualified failure in both cases leads to the conclusion that many narcissus species, and certainly those of the *jonquilla* section, should be kept dry in summer. I draw the line at annual lifting: bulbous irises are bother enough. If bulbs die away in the garden even with exceptional care, it appears that they are subjects for the alpine house and therefore beyond the scope of this book. With the utmost regret I must surrender the tiny jonquils—*calcicola, juncifolius, rupicola, watieri*—and turn to the few miniature narcissus that persist in the open and flower whenever the vagaries of winter weather permit.

NARCISSUS ASTURIENSIS was discussed in Chapter 6 since it is reliable enough to escape the gambler's category. It is not a rampant grower by any means but will maintain itself and increase sedately in a congenial spot. One of my bulbs prospered to the extent of producing four flowers. By that standard, when compared to the little jonquils, N. *asturiensis* is a rugged performer. In all likelihood its taste for shade and moist soil make it adapt to the humid New York summers that destroy the little *jonquillas*.

NARCISSUS of the *bulbocodium* section, the hoop petticoat daffodils, have followed an evolutionary detour that leads them to unique modifications, totally at odds with conventional daffodil design. Whether these changes constitute advance or backsliding is a matter of dispute among geneticists. To the unscientific eye the most drastic transformation is in the trumpet: instead of a tube, it becomes a funnel, a morning glory, two thirds of a globe, or a saucerlike ruffle. The perianth that forms a conspicuous halo in orthodox daffodils is reduced to flyaway apron strings. Leaves are dark green, thready, and may be profuse or limited to one or two.

Varieties of *Narcissus bulbocodium vulgaris*, the most commonly grown hoop petticoats, are neither difficult nor especially early. There are, however, two zany little bulbocodiums from the Atlas Mountains of Morocco which will actually bloom in midwinter whenever a thaw permits.

NARCISSUS BULBOCODIUM MONOPHYLLUS (CLUSII) FOLIOSUS is the earlier, sometimes blooming before the end of November. It looks like a cross between a daffodil and a wind sock and is about as tall as its name stood endwise. It is milk white in color with a severely tailored outline that would make it a suitable buttonhole for the Tin Woodman of Oz. In a sand bed at the foot of the south wall in Manhasset, a modest trial order of four bulbs increased in three years to the point of crowding. They yielded a heaping handful of dividends ranging in size from a grain of rice to a small acorn.

The bulbs came to me as *N. b. m. (c.) foliosus* (to take a short cut) and will probably continue to be listed in catalogues under that name. Synge however declares that the plant should be called *N. b. cantabricus foliosus*. Since the poor mite seems to acquire its staggering title by accretion, you can add *cantabricus* to the string if you like. With such a clutter of ascriptions, it's hardly necessary to point out that the genus needs a new and definitive monograph.

NARCISSUS BULBOCODIUM ROMIEUXII is infinitely prettier than *foliosus*. Its lavishly ruffled crinolines are light citron yellow and so widely flared that they press together like a crowd of extras dressing for *Gone With the Wind*. Unluckily *romieuxii* tries to flower in late January and early February, in recent years the beginning of our worst winter weather. If buds are exposed to subfreezing weather for weeks before a thaw allows them to open, the flowers are apt to be puny and flattened as if they had been pinched in a swinging door.

Sometimes prolonged cold will hold flowering back until the beginning of March. In that case *romieuxii* can put on its beguiling show without distortion, but on the whole the break of the weather favors the earlier *foliosus*.

If I should ever have a southern garden, I would give these quaint charmers a congenial home, adding the hybrid 'Nylon' and the lovely ruffled white *monophyllus* and *petunioides*, rated too tender for the North.

NARCISSUS CYCLAMINEUS is the clown of the family with trumpet so narrow and perianth so acutely reflexed that the flower looks as if it had been drawn nose first through a keyhole. It is deep yellow, early, reputed to seed freely in damp places, and refuses to grow for me. None of my authorities questions the hardiness of *N. cyclamineus*; my moist woods should have been exactly to its taste. In spite of my consistent failure I urge anyone with a sense of fun to try this fetching bit of floral nonsense.

NARCISSUS TAZETTA CANALICULATUS is a replica of the familiar bunch-flowered hybrids reduced to one-tenth their size but endowed with a full measure of their powerful scent. *N. t. canaliculatus* is daintiness itself when it first opens, standing about 5″ tall and carrying four to six flowers with yellow cups and reflexed white perianths. The scape stretches out in rather ungainly fashion as it ages, and the leaves grow out of all proportion and last until you're thoroughly tired of them. These are minor faults. The basic difficulty with *canaliculatus* is that it splits up into innumerable chips that pack the ground and make it impossible for any to grow to flowering size. I have tried separating and replanting the chips but find most of them too small to survive on their own. Deep planting, the method recommended for keeping tulip bulbs intact, was no better success. *Canaliculatus* is a most appealing miniature. I wish some way could be devised to keep it from multiplying itself out of existence.

It's stimulating to gamble with borderline plants if you accept the risk, and enormous satisfaction if you win. On the other hand, when you move an alpine to an impossibly alien soil and climate and stifle it with contaminated city air, it's unjust to blame the plant if it succumbs. Taking a gamble now and then is a good test of skill and luck, but the backbone of every garden is made up of reliable plants, the good growers that persist and increase without special nursing.

9

Summer Dress for Winter Bulbs

The winter garden relies chiefly on flowering bulbs. In planning for summer interest, the primary consideration must be the safety and welfare of these bulbs in dormancy.

The term "dormant" is somewhat misleading: bulbs are by no means inactive even though there is no evidence of life above ground. Leaves have disappeared but the food they manufactured is being utilized for vegetative increase and for the development of embryo buds for next season's bloom. Roots still take up water and dissolved nutrients: their territory must be guarded against rapacious competitors. Carpeting plants to cover the bare spaces left by the bulbs should be restricted to those with shallow roots.

It is a curious circumstance that rock gardens, surely the most refined specialty in outdoor horticulture, are beset by voracious weeds, not all of them vegetable. Lay one rock upon another and people will rush to share their infestation of sedums, johnny-jump-ups, ajuga, spurge, or invasive creepers. The compulsion is ruthless: I knew one woman who, undeterred by refusal, planted her weeds in an undefended rockery while the owner was away on vacation. It may seem harsh, but to protect your investment of time and backache in building a rockery, avoid unnamed handouts as you would a gift of measles. Accept the basket politely, put it in the shade, and see that it goes out with the garbage when the donor has left.

Before I go on to recommend desirable bulb covers and carpeting plants, I should warn beginners specifically about the commonest giveaways. It's tempting, I know, to fill the yawnings gaps of the newly constructed rockery with rapid-growing plants to get an immediate effect. If you do, you can forget the idea of replacing them with choicer plants. Once the weeds get a toehold, a blowtorch won't rout them.

SEDUMS undoubtedly head the list of garden menaces. Anyone who has sedums has too many and is eager to unload a bushel, as there's nothing so gratifying as giving away something you don't want anyway.

Sedums seed incontinently and can't be eradicated by pulling: they go to pieces at a touch and any fragment left on the soil will start a new colony.

There's little chance that you'll be offered one of the few good sedums, as these don't increase fast enough to need discarding, so I will say at the outset that anything that even resembles a sedum should be shunned like the plague it probably is.

VIOLETS and their kinfolk, the garden violas and johnny-jump-ups, are disarmingly modest flowers but behind each innocent face lurks an accomplished sharpshooter. In bloom most of the summer, their barrage of seed seems to pinpoint without fail the choicest of petit-point cushions, *Bellium bellioides* or *Gypsophila cerastioides*. By the time the violet leaves are big enough to give the alarm, their roots have anchored themselves so forcefully that the host plant must be lifted and pulled to pieces to extract the invader. Don't let minute size deceive you: among the worst offenders are VV. *jooi* and *nana*, tiny enough for a dollhouse windowbox and rampant as influenza.

LILY OF THE VALLEY is one of the foremost joys of spring when it hangs out its chime of scented bells. It also has stolons quite capable of burrowing under a sidewalk and establishing a beachhead on the other side. If it manages to infiltrate surface-rooting shrubs such as rhododendrons or skimmias, lily of the valley can be quite as damaging as pachysandra. Obviously such an invasive plant should be kept far from rock gardens or other select plantings.

Spring would be poor, however, without a generous bed of lily of the valley to pick by the fragrant handful. (I can feel as I write the initial resistance and then the sliding free of the angled stem.) If you haven't a rough corner where the plant can spread without encroaching on its betters, then look for an escape-proof container. I had such a spot in Tenafly, a foot-wide strip between driveway and house foundation which I interplanted with lily of the valley and Christmas fern, *Polystichum acrostichoides*, for winter ornament. When last seen, the two rugged performers were each holding its own against the other's aggression.

MYRTLE (*Vinca minor*) is a fine cover for banks and hard-luck places. It endures shade, is evergreen, durable, and really quite charming when its soft violet-blue flowers float above it like haze on distant hills. In theory myrtle should be easy to control simply by cutting back its surface runners. These have a sneaky way of insinuating themselves under a creeper where they escape notice. By the time new growth rises above their host, their roots are halfway to China. Once entrenched in the crevices of a rock wall, myrtle takes such a tenacious grip that if you attempt to pull it out, it will be the wall that gives.

I hope I have scared you enough to impress an inflexible rule: accept gift plants only if they have a verifiable scientific name. If you are offered two unfamiliar but named plants, for example *Potentilla villosa* and *P. alba*, you can check their habits and merits in reference book or catalogue and be guided to welcome the first and reject the second. If you admit plants with names like Gill-over-the-ground, Creeping Char-

ley, or Galloping Gertie, you're a lifetime member of the legion
of weed gardeners.

Now let us turn from weeds to the more agreeable subject
of desirable plants for the rock garden. Because of the great
number of worthy candidates, I think it will make for clarity
if I discuss the essential carpeting plants in this chapter and
keep accent plants for the next. As I go along I will specify
creepers whose restrained habit and shallow root system make
them suitable for bulb covers.

Strong-growing creepers have their place also. They are
necessary to disguise the joints between pieced-together rocks
and to prevent erosion in gullies between boulders. The dwarf
candytuft, *Iberis sempervirens* 'Pygmaea,' is top choice, with
Saponaria ocymoides and *Gypsophila repens* lagging behind
only because they are less compact. Descriptions of these
sturdy performers will be found in the alphabetical list that
follows.

ANACYCLUS DEPRESSUS is a delicate-looking trailer
with finely cut, yarrowlike leaves, hardly more than a green
filigree lacing over the chips of the moraine. The thready
stems bear relatively large daisies of singular coloring: pure
white above, dark red on the reverse, a striking contrast when
buds and open flowers are displayed together.

I was captivated by *Anacyclus depressus* when I first saw it
in the alpine garden of Stonecrop Nurseries at the International Flower Show in New York. As a native of Morocco its
hardiness might be suspect but Rex Murfitt, a director of the
nursery, assured me that it seeds freely enough to replace any
plants that winterkill and added that it wants light soil and
full sun. Aside from the fresh charm of its bicolored daisies,
a long period of summer bloom puts *Anacyclus depressus*
high on the list of plants I long to try if I have another garden.

ANDROSACES are among the choicest of alpines.
Their winter rosettes are so silvery and symmetrical that they

might almost be mistaken for encrusted saxifrages, though the androsaces' whiteness is due to silky hairs and not to beads of lime. While encrusted saxifrages are virtually impossible to keep in a lowland climate, androsaces are surprisingly tolerant and will even endure city conditions, surely a far cry from their native Himalayas. To make their site congenial, give them sun, a deep root run, gritty soil with some lime, and the sharpest possible drainage. A mulch of stone chips is advisable to keep the woolly rosettes from contact with damp earth.

ANDROSACE LANUGINOSA has rosettes so thickly furred that they appear almost pure white. In spring the plant develops long trailing stems, silver-leafed and bearing during the summer large umbels of pink flowers fading to white. A. *l. leichtlinii* has yellow- and red-eyed flowers in the same head, a distinction that would be noticed only by a keen observer. Pretty as the fringe of flowering stems may be, they have the defect of being brittle and are easily bent or broken by wind or careless handling.

ANDROSACE SARMENTOSA and A. PRIMULOIDES are very similar: some authorities consider A. *primuloides* a variety of *sarmentosa*. Both are neater, more self-contained than the trailing A. *lanuginosa* and have even more beautiful winter rosettes, so thickly webbed that they have the sheen of brushed silver. As leaves expand in growth, the underlying light green becomes more apparent but always veiled with silky down.

In May the center of the rosette rises on a short stem and unfolds into a prim little parasol of pink flowers with light yellow centers, a perfect miniature of its cousin, *Primula malacoides*. The method of increase is like a strawberry's: the plant sends out numerous short runners, each rooting at the tip and producing an infant rosette. These are easily moved to any ledge or crevice in the rocks that needs a distinguished ornament.

ARABIS STURII is probably a dwarf form of the
rather coarse and open-growing A. *procurrens*. Its glossy, dark
green leaves form a solid mat about an inch deep and nearly
evergreen. The white flowers in loose racemes are not of top
quality and may well be shorn to preserve the smooth surface
of the carpet.

Arabis sturii is too assertive to be used as cover for the
tiniest bulbs, though it makes an excellent setting for tall,
strong-growing crocuses such as *C. chrysanthus* 'E. A.
Bowles' and *C. tomasinianus* 'Whitewell Purple.' Snowdrops and dwarf tulips look especially well when grown
through *Arabis sturii* which matches their larger scale and enhances by contrast the frosty bloom of their leaves.

ARENARIA LARICIFOLIA is a plant of obscure origin
but uncommon charm. Except that its bristly cushion is light
green instead of blue-gray, it might be mistaken for a cousin
dianthus. Certainly its finely slashed white flowers on wiry
stems are very close to those of *Dianthus noeanus*, but the
arenaria is smaller, neater, and more compact. *Arenaria laricifolia* differs from dianthus in liking acidity but agrees with
them in a preference for sun and sandy soil.

AUBRIETA DELTOIDEA is one of the indispensable
rock plants, as highly valued for its billows of gray-green foliage as for the profusion of purple flowers that cover the mat
from April to June. It makes an ideal bulb cover: rooting is
shallow, the creeping stems so thready that they permit aeration of the soil, yet the mat is dense enough to prevent splattering by mud in driving rainstorms. Even the rather touchy
Narcissus asturiensis has increased well under A. *deltoidea*.
Both the tiny daffodil and the hosts of yellow crocus species
that accompany it are flattered by the aubrieta's purple-flow-
ered carpet.

In addition to its service as bulb cover, aubrieta looks its best when it pours smoothly over a rock, following its contour and breaking into a foam of new growth where it roots again at the bottom. It is particularly attractive when its soft mats fan out over the walk at the foot of the rockery.

Since aubrietas are so desirable for their foliage and their long season of bloom, their named varieties should be searched out and tried for a change of color. I once had a very beautiful one called 'Gloriosa' with flowers twice the size of *deltoidea's* and of a delightfully luminous shade of candy pink. Never a fast increaser, it survived the move to New Jersey but gradually dwindled away. I believe the shift to clay soil was inimical, and probably also the shade from distant trees to south and west. If I have 'Gloriosa' again I will give it grittier soil and a mulch of stone chips.

Sturdy *Aubrieta deltoidea* needs no pampering, growing amiably in any prepared rock garden soil. When it finishes blooming, it should be clipped over severely. This may leave some temporary bald spots but new growth will soon fill them in and keep the mat as dense and uniform as it should be.

BELLIUM BELLIOIDES is an engaging little plant, prim and funny. Though described as a creeper, with me it humped its tiny, dark green, spoon-shaped leaves into a close tuffet. The plant is said to like lime: perhaps the lack of it in my predominantly acid gardens curtailed its spread. I am content to have it stay as round and solid as a pincushion which it so comically resembles when studded all over with minute white daisies on hairlike 2" stems.

Perhaps if *Bellium bellioides* crept as it is supposed to do, I could use it as a bulb cover, but I shouldn't think of disrupting its neat cushion by letting bulb foliage spear through it.

CAMPANULAS are a diverse race, ranging from that slouching villain *C. rapunculoides* to the most treasured alpine jewels. Many of the choice species grow in full sun in rock crevice or scree, sinking a taproot deep into recesses cooled by melting snow from the slopes above. From the root, long stolons push to the surface, placing new rosettes sometimes at considerable distances from the parent.

Obviously it's impossible to reproduce alpine conditions in the sultry lowlands. Fortunately campanulas are quite adaptable. If you do your best to suit them, the plants will meet you more than halfway.

The primary objective is to keep crowns sunny and dry while roots are cool and moist. A deep channel between ledge rocks is ideal both aesthetically and functionally. Directions for constructing and planting a crevice are given in the first chapter.

If ledge rock isn't available, the cooling effect of a deeply sunken rock can be utilized. A smaller rock may be set close to the first one so that the campanulas will be marshaled in a little valley for greater concentration. Admittedly their airy bells are more effective when they spring away from a nearly vertical rock face, yet I would rather have campanulas next to a boulder than none at all. Give them gritty, alkaline soil with some humus below. If campanulas are grown in the open, a mulch of stone chips will protect their creeping roots from baking in the sun.

Blue flowers are rare, and rock plants that bloom in midsummer rarer still. Campanulas have both virtues with daintiness and beauty for good measure—surely reasons enough to justify the effort needed to make them feel at home.

No two authorities agree on the nomenclature of campanulas, so it follows that they are muddled in commerce. I will try to indicate the aliases under which the finest ones may appear in catalogues.

CAMPANULA COCHLEARIFOLIA (syn. *pusilla*) is a delicate creeper, spreading widely when it can get its roots into a cool, limy crevice. Toothed leaves form a mat about an inch high, concealed for most of the summer by a cloud of fairy thimbles on 3″ stems. The type is light blue-violet; there is a charming but scarce albino. C. c. 'Miranda' has larger but paler bells, more silver-gray than blue. I had a superb form called 'Miranda' Lohbrunner Form, taller and much deeper blue than the type. Among its profusion of dancing bells, some nodded and some turned upward, giving a delightful air of animation.

CAMPANULA DASYANTHA is a native of Alaska and the Aleutian Islands, and obviously calls for the full scree-with-humus-reservoir treatment. Since it flowers in July it will benefit from additional coolness on broiling days. A canvas soil soaker, though a drippy nuisance to handle, is the best way to supply a continuous trickle of cold water to the roots without wetting the crowns.

I am not sure whether *Campanula dasyantha* is beautiful or merely strange. It forms a low mat of almost prostrate, glossy, leather-textured leaves. Above this on short stems rise preposterously large flowers: violet tubes as big as your thumb, stiffly upright, flaring at the mouth and furnished inside with glistening white hairs. Without the evidence of photographs, I would find it hard to believe that this outlandish alpine grew well in a lowland garden.

CAMPANULAS ELATINES, FENESTRELLATA, and GARGANICA are disputed by monographers and utterly confused in the trade. L. H. Bailey and H. Clifford Crook, both authorities on the genus, declare that one is the species and the others merely varieties of it. As they differ on which is which, I will follow the RHS *Dictionary of Gardening* which shows no partiality but lists them all as separate species.

The three are similar in appearance, all having racemes of flat, starry flowers of various intensities of blue-violet. The most compact, and my first choice, is C. *fenestrellata*, distinguished from the others by the high gloss of its foliage. Its tufts of shining dark green leaves with strongly recurved teeth are an ornament in their own right, and form a mat dense enough to keep soil from washing. The racemes of flowers lie flat against the compressed foliage, making a refined but vigorous carpet for a steep ravine or valley between rocks.

CC. *elatines* and *garganica* have downy leaves. *Elatines* supposedly has three flowers to a stem while *garganica* has one or two, a seemingly flimsy means of distinction. *Elatines* is procumbent; *garganica* larger and more erect. *Garganica* looks like a smaller, neater, and more richly colored *poscharskyana*, but without the running roots that make the last so invasive.

CAMPANULA PORTENSCHLAGIANA (syn. *muralis*) is a first-rate plant, a slowly spreading mat of shining notched leaves. The upturned flowers are rich violet in color, bell-shaped at the base, then opening into a collar of five rounded lobes. Deep tone and broad surface make for greater concentration of color than the narrow-lobed stars of the *elatines* group can offer. For garden effect, *portenschlagiana* tops the list of easily grown campanulas.

Campanula portenschlagiana is handicapped by a formidable name and by confusion with C. *poscharskyana*, a sprawling, sickly-colored weed with a highly offensive odor. If you will remember that posch is bosh, there will be no chance of your ordering the wrong plant.

Portenschlagiana could have been worse, at that. It was named for an Austrian collector, Father Edler von Portenschlag-Ledermayer.

CAMPANULA RAINERI is an uncommon species that deserves wider distribution. The flowers are upfacing bowls with five pointed scallops around the brim, and are of a pleasing shade of clear blue-violet. The flower might be mistaken for a very dwarf C. *carpatica* but the resemblance goes no further. *Carpatica* is a rowdy plant, big and floppy, whereas *raineri* is the essence of refinement. Its neat, gray-dusted rosettes compare favorably with an androsace's. In July when the relatively enormous flowers stand above them on 3" stems, the plant is unrivaled for charm.

Campanula raineri spreads by underground stolons and therefore needs a loose, gritty soil to roam in, with humus below to maintain a supply of moisture.

DIANTHUS provide the rock garden with some of its finest cushions, made up of spiky leaves yet plump and bouncy to the touch. They revel in the driest, sunniest, sandiest spot in your garden where few alpines could survive. The soil for dianthus should be well limed; a mulch of stone chips will insure that no slug-attracting dampness can linger under their flounces.

Since the cushions, out of bloom, are flat and featureless, they will gain interest if planted on a hummocky slope or forced to wind their way among the rocks of a dry stream bed.

Most of the familiar species are too large for a supporting role as carpet for a winter garden. One of the suitable miniatures is *Dianthus neglectus*, with bright pink flowers, buffy on the underside, just 2" above its tufts of grassy leaves. 'Dawn' is a fine hybrid, a little larger in scale but very striking in the contrast between its blue-green foliage and clear pink flowers with glowing red eye.

My top favorite for the select rock garden is 'Tiny Rubies,' an enchanting mite with gray-green mat and perfectly formed double carnations, rosy crimson in color, spicily scented, and all of ¼" across. Dainty as it is, 'Tiny Rubies' is a strong grower and will in time make a mat 12" or more wide, a spread which is out of proportion to the diminutive flowers. When it exceeds its bounds, 'Tiny Rubies' should be clipped back and the cuttings rooted for admiring friends—one safe exception to the rule against handouts.

DRYAS OCTOPETALA is one of the choicest Western American alpines. A prostrate shrublet with gnarled, twisted trunk, it has a look of great antiquity. Its evergreen leaves are edged with neat rounded scallops, almost beadlike; the undersides are powdered white. The large flowers look like upright cherry blossoms, creamy white and centered with a fluff of gold stamens. When bloom is past, the stem lengthens and produces a vast flyaway seed head, as furry as those of clematis or pulsatilla and quite unlike anything you'd expect of a member of the rose family.

Dryas octopetala is a plant of high altitudes. The higher it grows, the larger and more full-petaled the flowers. Around 6000 feet the flowers are the size of a quarter and mostly have the regulation eight segments. About 7500 feet up the western flank of the Victoria Range, on the ice-rimmed shore of Lake Oesa, the dryas flowers would have overlapped a half dollar. Though it was early August, the air was so piercingly cold that it was painful to pull gloves off long enough to take a picture. Seeing the plants in their chosen environment, a windswept rock shelf as bleak as the face of the moon, it was difficult to believe that dryas will grow on Long Island's sand bar close to sea level.

Obviously such a treasure needs a setting. Since it grows above timber line, dryas must have no overhead shade, but instead should get its roots deep in a cool crevice or between half-buried rocks. Soil should be gritty and alkaline and must never become parched. A thick dressing of stone chips will shade the soil and reduce evaporation.

GLOBULARIA NANA is one of the smallest of evergreen shrubs, growing no more than an inch high. Its deep green leaves, in shape like miniature ice tea spoons, form such a compressed mound that no woody stem is visible. In June fuzzy balls of bloom sit just above the mound and would be charming if they were a better color. Unfortunately theirs is such a watered tint of ash blue that they appear faded, looking in fact more like seed heads than fresh flowers.

Despite its shortcoming as a flowering plant, the little shrub is a most refined ornament for a prominent ledge or crevice. The standard formula—full sun, sharp drainage, gritty lime soil—is recommended.

GYPSOPHILA CERASTIOIDES is a tufted plant, spreading slowly into a compact mound 2″ to 3″ high. The spoon-shaped leaves are midgreen so heavily coated with downy hairs that they appear gray. The flowers, relatively large and sitting close to the mat, are white with pink, red, or purple veining.

Gypsophila cerastioides roots deeply and therefore is not recommended as a bulb cover. For a native of the Himalayas, it is surprisingly tough, standing heat, dryness, and even city conditions. It wants well-limed soil and full sun. G. *cerastioides* is a well-mannered plant, especially appealing to gardeners who like unusual plants that need no fussing over.

GYPSOPHILA REPENS is a fast spreader, certainly no plant for the pocket handkerchief garden but one to remember in case you ever have to mask a dump. Its thready blue stems and tiny pink flowers make a 6″ mat as fine as a cloud of veiling, so airy that it escapes the coarseness of, say, the blatant mustard, *Alyssum saxatile*. Because of its loose texture it makes a good cover for tulips or daffodils, even the large garden hybrids.

HELIOSPERMA ALPESTRE FL.-PL. (syn. *Silene alpestris fl.-pl.*) is both creeper and flowering accent, so valuable that it merits praise in both categories. It spreads by underground shoots to form a dark green, rather open mat about 2″ high. I would have thought it too robust for a bulb cover but the heliosperma proved its own suitability: it crept so gently over dormant bulb plantings that I was unaware of the trespass until crocuses bloomed unharmed among its shoots.

Heliosperma alpestre holds the record for longest continual bloom of any herbaceous perennial I have grown. From its peak in late May and early June, it is never without a scattering of flowers until mid-November. Its double white flowers, deeply cleft and touched with green in the center, are carried on wiry, wide-branching stems 6″ above the mats. The airy sprays suggest the Baby's Breath that used to be grown as a vase stuffer, but on a much neater scale.

Beyond the usual need for sun, good drainage, and open soil, heliosperma offers no problems. In placing the plants, take advantage of the spraylike effect of the flowers as they spring into the air on their almost invisible stems. If you have a staircase of ledges, a steep ravine, or a vertical fault that in nature would channel a brook, let the heliosperma flowers mimic a little fall of water foaming down the rocks.

HOUSTONIA COERULEA is the bluet that mists the eyes of those who studied under New England elms. Wherever seen, they recall the impetuous onrush of spring, the roar of swollen brooks, the ecstatic shrilling of peepers in every hollow, and the bowl of South Campus brimming with bluets.

Houstonia coerulea grows in tufts about 2″ high and spreads both by seed and by runners. Its flowers stand high enough to top the winter grass, each on its hairlike stem, facing up to show a four-pointed star of clear blue-violet with a yellow eye rimmed in white. The bluet likes a great deal of moisture—I have seen it flourishing on stream banks and on mossy rock faces glistening with seeping water—but it will grow in a low spot of the rock garden if the soil is crammed with leafmold and well watered during periods of drought.

HOUSTONIA SERPYLLIFOLIA is even more refined, a creeper with tiny round leaves, so prostrate that it is no more than a film of green. It grew poorly on my dry Manhasset hilltop, seldom flowering and dying away in disfiguring brown patches.

Either bluet would make an ideal bulb cover as far as restraint and shallow rooting are concerned, but I fear that bulbs would suffer from the large amounts of water needed to keep the bluets from burning.

HYDROCOTYLE PEDUNCULARIS is such an inconsiderable thing that I wonder why anyone bothered to bring it all the way from Tasmania. Its chief interest, in fact, is that it adds a name to the list of subequatorial plants that will grow in the North.

Hydrocotyle peduncularis makes an inch-high mat of shiny round leaves with scalloped edges, a little like those of a wrong-end-of-the-telescope nasturtium. It makes a nice filler for cracks in paving stones or for any moist place where its spread can be controlled. Innocuous as it is above ground, hydrocotyle has forceful, far-ranging stolons which are hard to eradicate if they get a foothold under some choicer mat.

IBERIS SEMPERVIRENS 'PYGMAEA' is no more than 4" high, compact, uniform, and as different from the sprawling common candytuft as velvet from marsh grass. To be sure, the common candytuft can be whacked back to 4", but the bare stubs and litter of dead stems are unsightly until new growth covers them. 'Pygmaea' never needs shearing, though its spent flower heads may be clipped off so that the tiny-leafed shrub can be seen at its best.

Curiously enough, 'Pygmaea' seems to grow only at the ends: an established plant is loaf-shaped, not round. This obliging eccentricity makes 'Pygmaea' an ideal subject for concealing an awkward gap between rocks as well as securing exposed soil against washing.

LOTUS PINNATUS is the horticultural alias of a plant of baffling identity. Since its pinnate leaves have too many leaflets for a lotus, it must be a hosackia, but diligent search has failed to turn up a form as prostrate as this one. By any name, it is a tremendously strong grower: a push on its thick mat meets the resistance of a block of wood. Like *Iberis* 'Pygmaea,' *Lotus pinnatus* makes a tough and effective soil holder.

In May its dark green cushion is ornamented with whorls of bright yellow pea flowers, a cheery and eye-catching display. Though *L. pinnatus* roots deeply, I tried growing *Crocus speciosus* under it with the hope that the crocus's long flimsy tubes might find support. While the crocus's naked flowers looked charming above their borrowed petticoat, they flopped as badly as ever, plainly needing a taller prop than the ground-hugging lotus could provide.

MINUARTIA VERNA CAESPITOSA (syn. *Arenaria caespitosa*) looks at first glance like a mat of bristly, brilliant green moss. Unlike moss, however, it is studded with starry white flowers in early spring and requires full sun.

Though *Minuartia verna caespitosa* is too rampant a grower for the rock garden, it makes an excellent heavy-duty bulb cover for open situations. I used it extensively in sunny portions of the wild garden where it could spread without endangering frailer plants. Leafless autumnal crocuses in particular gain by growing through minuartia, as their delicate colors are enhanced by a background of greenery.

Minuartia grows so vigorously that parts of it are pushed up into hummocks. This is an asset in the case of the tall *Crocus speciosus* varieties, as several inches of their long tubes may be concealed by the minuartia's billowy mounds. If minuartia grows so luxuriantly that shorter bulbs are likely to be swamped, it is easy to pluck out the surplus and let the space fill again with flat new growth.

MUEHLENBECKIA AXILLARIS makes a 2″ mat of hair-thin stems and tiny, sparse, round leaves. It is advertised as a bulb cover but to my mind is too thin to cover anything—too thin, certainly, to choke out weed seeds which find safe lodging in its tangle of runners. A native of New Zealand, muehlenbeckia is of interest only to collectors.

NIEREMBERGIA RIVULARIS is another subequatorial plant, this time from Argentina and a gem of the first water—no idle figure, for it must have a site that is consistently moist. From June to autumn its carpet of deep green leaves is studded with upright bells, very large, almost stemless, and suggesting one of the rare alpine campanulas except for their color, which is creamy white with yellow at the base. Nierembergia would be most at home along the stones of a brookside, but it will grow at the lowest point of a rockery if given almost pure leafmold and plenty of water.

PHLOX SUBULATA has been called Mountain Pink, Creeping Phlox, or Gas Station Pink—the last, as it refers to the common magenta form, being most to the point. This is one of the blights perpetuated not by seed but by handouts, like unwanted kittens.

A good rousing carmine can be literally stunning when set off by rose-pink, white, and green, as a grouping of Japanese peonies will evidence. The owners of *Phlox subulata* seem vaguely aware that its doleful, faded magenta is unsatisfactory so they liven it up with taxicab yellow *Alyssum saxatile* and scarlet tulips. The result is hailed as a Riot of Color, a term non-gardeners consider complimentary.

Because the common *Phlox subulata* lends itself so readily to tooth-grating discords, discriminating gardeners wince at mere mention of the name. There are however some worthy forms, slow-growing, compact, and agreeably colored, which it would be a loss to overlook. 'Arbutus' for one is a neat plant with tiny pale pink flowers, as dainty as its namesake. 'Blue

Hills' is well named: its hazy violet-blue is paler than one could wish but it is attractive when grown beside a yellow-flowering creeper such as *Potentilla villosa. Rosea,* or *douglasii rosea,* is nonspreading and bears soft deep pink flowers over a long season. 'Snow Queen' is a low and compact white. I once had an outstanding form called 'Camla' (or *camlaensis* or *nivalis camla* as it appeared in different catalogues). It was rather loose-growing and not too vigorous but I recall the exceptional size and beauty of its clear pink flowers in spring and again in autumn.

The creeping phloxes like gritty acid soil in full sun, and the sharp drainage that goes with a raised position in the rock garden.

POTENTILLA CINEREA is a rugged yet restrained creeper whose twisted, prostrate stems repeat the contours of the rocks they grow over. The dark, slashed foliage is handsome at all times and in May serves as a foil for showers of shiny buttercups on 2″ stems. These are not stiffly upright but slant in the direction of growth so that each promontory of the mat is outlined with a fringe of gold flowers.

Potentilla cinerea is not fussy about soil so long as it is not extremely acid. The thick stems will rot in prolonged wet periods, especially when resting in winter. Sharp drainage is essential and, for good measure, a thick layer of stone chips will raise the crown of the plant above possible contact with damp soil.

POTENTILLA VILLOSA is a first-rate creeper, capable of covering a large area yet easily kept in bounds. Its close mat of frosty blue cinquefoil leaves is outstandingly beautiful unadorned and quite enchanting when spangled with clear yellow flowers. Although a native of Alaska, *P. villosa* is amazingly tolerant of lowland conditions, even thriving

in the city—in fact, I find it difficult to say enough in praise of
a plant that is neither scarce nor difficult.

Potentilla villosa is shallow-rooted and would make a good
bulb cover, yet its flowering carpet is too delightful to be
topped by ripening leaves. Though the plant is essentially a
creeper, I like to isolate a few rooted runners of *villosa* and let
them grow into small mounds, for their oddly blue leaves and
prim flowers remind me of the little tufted plants in the foreground of a tapestry.

SAPONARIA OCYMOIDES is a vigorous trailer forming
a tangled mat 6" to 8" high. Despite overall size, its compo-
nents are so dainty and its growth so open and airy that it
never appears coarse or lumpish. When covered with a froth of
candy pink flowers, *S. ocymoides* might be mistaken for a
creeping phlox, but its habit has far more individuality. Instead of the phlox's featureless prickly mat, *ocymoides* is a
tumble of red-purple stems and small gray-green leaves, making an interesting pattern even when not in bloom—which is
seldom, for the saponaria flowers profusely in early May and
then on and off during most of the summer whenever the notion takes it.

Like *Gypsophila repens*, *Saponaria ocymoides* is too rampant to turn loose in a small rockery. Nevertheless it should be
kept in mind for emergencies an androsace or dryas would be
too small to cope with. More than once when hunting material for a rockery, I have dug up a rock long buried in woods
soil or under a blanket of rotting leaves. Stained by tannin
and earth minerals, the rock appeared to be the same dark tone
as the rest of my collection. After a year's exposure, the stain
washed off to show an obtrusive face of light tan. Rather than
tear down the rockery to remove the offender, it can easily be
concealed behind a valance of *Saponaria ocymoides*—but remember the plant's roving proclivities and keep its spread in
check.

SEDUMS, as I warned earlier, are mostly weeds. The two exceptions which I would admit to a cultivated area are *SS. cauticola* and *sieboldii*. Both are Japanese, both so exotic-looking, so artificial, that they would be out of place in a naturalistic setting. However in a frankly man-made construction —a retaining wall or rock garden bordering a terrace or against the foundation of a house—their form and color have a distinct fascination.

SEDUM CAUTICOLA is a notable subject for the front of the rockery. A lax plant, it will fringe the face of a rock and spread its heavy flower heads over the paving at its foot.

Sedum cauticola is a strange plant with purple stems and thick blue-green leaves that look more mineral than vegetable. The large flat heads of flowers are a rather harsh shade of deep rose, one that might be frowned on in the flush of summer. It is easier to be tolerant of a plant that begins to bloom in October, and in any case the color is quite harmonious with the soft blue-violets of the first autumnal crocuses.

Sedum cauticola seeds itself sparingly. The infants are at once advertised by their extraordinary color and can easily be removed if they come up where not wanted. Since the basal rosettes of the sedum, as well as its long streamers, are on the sparse side, the plants should be massed as closely as they can be crowded, an effect best realized by cramming the volunteer seedlings into any void that offers.

SEDUM SIEBOLDII looks like something a kindergartner might string together from soda straws and rounds of colored paper. The fat leaves are arranged in threes, so closely set that the stem appears to pierce them. The leaves are blue-gray with a silvery bloom, while their waved edges are tinted coral pink. *S. sieboldii* is a prettier plant than *cauticola*, as the stems have enough spring to arch into the air before drooping under the weight of their terminal flowers. These are smaller and rounder than *cauticola's*, with a fluffy look that adds lightness, and above all a softer and more pleasing shade of rose.

If grown in an open spot, *sieboldii* forms a wheel with flowers circling its rim. I rather prefer it backed against a ledge so that the stems are forced to spray out in the shape of a fan, thus doubling their fullness and gaining a lively irregularity in the disposition of the flowers.

SEMPERVIVUMS are the vegetable equivalent of cement, invaluable for chinking cracks between rocks and preventing erosion. They get along on almost no soil and water. I have a photograph of a colony growing in a hairline crevice in the vertical rock wall that framed the sunken garden in Manhasset. I can't imagine how they got there: they couldn't possibly have been deliberately planted in such a minute opening, and I always removed flowering stems before they could set seed. However they contrived to get a start, the rosettes flourished on whatever minerals they could obtain from aging cement, and presumably on moisture that seeped through the wall from the earth behind it.

Full sun and starvation diet are essential to sempervivums. Shade and rich living make them grow pale, bloated, and flabby. Make sure that they have a raised position with crumbled mortar rubble to root in—or failing that, well-limed sand and coarsely crushed stone.

The highly colored sempervivums are best displayed in a dry wall where their various shades of maroon, russet, and silvery green make beautiful patterns. These forms are too bulky for the small rock garden, and their grotesquely long flowering stems are even more out of scale.

SEMPERVIVUM ARACHNOIDEUM, the cobweb houseleek, forms dainty rosettes, closely packed and centered with a netting of fine white threads. The flowers are many-pointed stars of a curious tawny rose color, Tyrian pink by the chart, with darker midribs. Two rows of stamens with long red filaments, very like eyelashes, give a wide-awake look. Unlike the larger forms whose flowering shoots remind me of a mess of giant steamed clams, *S. arachnoideum* is more compact in habit though it may stretch to 5″ as the last flowers open.

If you value the sempervivum as a living mosaic, you may wish to twist out any rosette that starts to develop a flowering stem—or at least pluck it out when the aging shoot becomes ungainly. The rosettes die after flowering and must be removed in any case. If you wish to preserve the uniformity of the clump, it is best to pull out the fertile rosettes while they are still small.

THYMES come late in the alphabet but first in utility as bulb covers. They bloom in summer long after bulb foliage has ripened and disappeared, so their modest show is not diminished by straggly leaves. Except to the honeybees that swarm over them, flowers are secondary to the incomparable carpets of tiny leaves. Trailing stems weave a tight net, unhappily not squirrel-proof but requiring so much effort that the pests often get discouraged and go elsewhere for easier digging.

THYMUS SERPYLLUM varieties are the most desirable for bulb covers. The commonest forms are *albus, rosea*, and *coccinea*, with a few horticultural varieties such as the pale pink 'Annie Hall.' The woolly thyme, *T. s. lanuginosus*, has dark, faintly purple-tinged leaves covered with dull fuzz. It is a somber plant, rather dusty-looking, passable in small patches as a change of texture but to my eye lacking the freshness of the shining-leafed varieties. *T. s. conglomerata* seems to be a garden form not recognized in reference books. Its congested branches, 2″ to 3″ high, are crammed with bright green leaves. The slight irregularity of its surface makes a pleasant diversion from the unrelieved flatness of the other *serpyllum* varieties.

Apart from serving as bulb covers, the prostrate creeping thymes are valuable for softening the joints of sand-laid flagstone walks. *T. s. albus* is delightful in paving, as its light green leaves and stemless white flowers spread over the stones in a pattern as intricate and fine as a lace doily. In theory the thyme should be trodden on to release its pungent fragrance, but guests tiptoed around it with the utmost care, and I could never bring myself to trample the delicate filigree.

THYMUS HERBA-BARONA is sometimes advertised as a rock plant but it is too untidy and too aggressive for a select spot. It grows about 8″ high, a most unsightly tangle of wiry stems and sickly lavender flowers. Nevertheless its caraway scent is so delicious that it might be given an out-of-the-way spot, perhaps at the edge of the barbecue area where it can be firmly stepped on during cooking, or, if nothing better suggests itself, beside the garbage can.

VERONICAS supply the most radiant blues of any easily grown rock garden perennials—not the retiring blue-violets of campanulas but bold hues approaching gentian and lobelia. The identification of veronicas, especially of the dwarf ones, is wavery in books and completely addled in the trade. Ordering them is equivalent to dipping into a grab bag. Fortunately the family standard is high: there are few weedy or inferior members, so the chance is excellent that you will be pleased with whatever the postman brings.

VERONICA REPENS is so distinct that it is not apt to be confused in commerce. I will risk the opinion that it forms the most beautiful carpet of any creeping plant: hardly half an inch high, dark green and shining, with little leaves so smoothly laid along the surface that they rival lizard scales for elegance. To round off its perfection, the mat is evergreen. While any sparse-leafed small bulbs will be enhanced by growing through it, I believe that white flowers gain most by contrast with its dark mat, and would reserve V. *repens* as a foil for snowdrops and the lovely *Crocus biflorus* 'White Lady.'

Though a native of Corsica, *Veronica repens* is quite hardy, slow-growing but dependable, and seems to have no fads about soil so long as it is reasonably well drained and in full sun.

The flowers of *Veronica repens* are not up to the superb quality of its foliage. Like those of *Globularia nana,* they are faded ash blue. I suggest that you clip them off or look the other way when the plant is blooming.

VERONICA RUPESTRIS is one of the most scrambled species, having been listed as V. *teuchrium, teuchrium dubia, prostrata,* and *teuchrium prostrata.* The plant most frequently sent out as *rupestris* forms a cushion of dark green, prickly foliage. In May it is covered with erect 6″ spikes of intense gentian blue, a most impressive concentration of color. The plant should be sheared after flowering to restore the neatness of the mat.

In addition to the singular blueness of its flowers, *Veronica rupestris* has the useful property of doubling for litmus paper. In soil that is excessively acid, the blue disappears, leaving a weak, soiled magenta that will send you running for the bag of ground limestone.

VERONICA RUPESTRIS NANA, again based on what informed dealers supply, is even better suited to the small rock garden. It is a decumbent plant, the fine-leafed stems turning upwards at their tips to display short spikes of royal blue flowers. This is not a creeper: its trailing stems radiate from the crown without rooting. Though it does not form a carpet for bulbs to grow through, the veronica's lengthening stems will cover the bare space left when bulbs go dormant.

Veronica rupestris nana is perhaps the most splendid saturation of blue available to the small garden (always excepting the alpine gentians which are intolerant of lowland conditions). It is a plant I hold in special affection, for it recalls the celestial carpets of veronicas that spread a blue turf below crimson paintbrush, erythroniums, and buttercups on the slopes of Mt. Rainier.

10

Fancy Free

The flatness of carpeting plants makes them excellent backgrounds for bulbs. It also makes for monotony. Once the sites of winter bulbs are covered with plants and thereby secured against accidental digging, the gardener is free to indulge a taste for drama. Taller plants for accent, others for striking foliage, above all those with showier flowers than the useful but unassuming thymes can muster—the choice is so boundless that only the very finest and most rewarding need be considered.

AETHIONEMA PULCHELLUM is an arresting shrublet, so blue that it appears painted. Its slender, many-branched stems twist in on themselves so that the plant stands no more than 5″ high. In midsummer its heads of bright pink flowers make a startling contrast against the blue of stems and foliage.

Aethionemas are plants for scrupulously tended gardens, for their thready growth is a beacon for weed seeds. Since they are slender, they should be planted closely so that their branches can interlace for maximum concentration of their singular color. They want gritty lime soil in full sun. Since aethionemas are on the borderline of hardiness in Zone 7a, it is prudent to root cuttings to keep in a cold frame over winter in case replacements are necessary.

AQUILEGIAS, at least the alpine species suitable for rock gardens, are unable to adapt to lowland conditions. The difficulty of growing alpines at low altitudes was outlined in the first chapter but details are worth repeating as they apply specifically to columbines. The lethal factor is not so much the heat of our summers as their duration, a point not often brought forward.

The alpine aquilegias are geared to a short growing season, framed between the retreat of snowbanks in July and the fresh snows of September. In the lowlands, aquilegias start into growth when the ground thaws, and bloom and set seed in April. Their business done for the year, they shed their leaves in anticipation of a ten-month sleep. Instead of snow, our summers pile on heat and more heat. The columbines manfully produce a new crop of leaves which in turn die away and must be replaced, each time more weakly until the plant dies of exhaustion. The prolonged distress of the aquilegias, evidenced by yellow leaves and feeble growth, quite outweighs the charm of their spring flowering.

For those who garden in cooler climates or higher altitudes, the small aquilegias AA. *akitensis, flabellata nana* and *f. n. alba* are delightful. I once had an entrancing dwarf called A. *jucunda,* a variety of A. *glandulosa.* It was a compact plant, under 6″, with relatively enormous flowers set just above the rich blue-green foliage. The short-spurred flowers had cream-colored tubes and violet skirts with a jaunty flare that banished any impression of stubbiness. I no longer see A. *jucunda* offered but it is a treasure to put high on your wish list.

ARMERIAS are among the most engaging of cushions, appearing in the list of accent plants rather than as bulb covers because they are too decorative, in or out of flower, to be obscured by ripening bulb foliage. All are gratifyingly generous with bloom—as Gerard said of them, "They floure from May, till Summer be farre spent." Because of their congested growth and fiber-thatched, prostrate stems, the sharpest possible drainage is imperative. Give them a raised position in full sun, a deep pocket of gritty lime soil, and a heavy mulch of stone chips to keep their crowns above soil level.

ARMERIA CAESPITOSA (syn. A. *juniperifolia*) is a pad of spiky leaves, dense and flat, with round heads of pink flowers that seem to have been patted onto the prickles. There is a white form and many hybrids, in the main larger and easier to keep than the type.

ARMERIA MARITIMA is a bolder plant with bright green, alliumlike leaves. Above the clump on 8" stems stand pink balls of flowers like jewel-headed hatpins. Brilliant carmine flowers make the variety A. *m. laucheana* even more eye-catching.

Even with the utmost precaution in providing perfect drainage, *Armeria maritima* is relatively short-lived. In prolonged spells of rain or melting snow, the thick mat gets sodden and takes as long to dry as a wet collie. After such unavoidable soakings, a whole section of a mature plant will suddenly turn brown. When you trace back the affected part, you find that its supporting stem has rotted close to the taproot. The rest of the plant usually follows suit so it is prudent to salvage the still living tips for cuttings. Be sure to snip off every trace of their shaggy, fibrous sheathing before inserting them in rooting medium.

ARMERIA SETACEA is a charming miniature resembling A. *caespitosa* but a little larger in scale. Its pincushion of pointed leaves is thickly studded with umbels of pink flowers, standing perhaps an inch above the mat. Like the others it must have rapid drainage and an open limy soil.

ATHYRIUM GOERINGIANUM PICTUM is a fern of such beautiful spring coloring that it almost rates as a flower. A native of Japan and the only hardy painted fern, it is worthy of a place in the most discriminating collection. The outer edges of the fronds are silvery, deepening to frosty green and then changing to muted pink as they approach the midribs, which are colored deep mulberry. The colors fade to a conventional fern green in summer, but the fronds are still ornamental if no longer spectacular.

Like *Veronica rupestris nana,* the athyrium's expanding leaves will cover a considerable area, especially if planted in groups of three or more. I grew my finest snowdrops, *Galanthus elwesii* and *G. nivalis* 'Samuel Arnott,' between clumps of the fern. The snowdrops flowered and completed their growth before the lengthening fronds overtook them, and seemed to be unaffected by the thick curtain that hung over their beds all summer.

Athyrium goeringianum pictum wants loose acid soil with a good measure of humus, and seems able to endure full sun if given water in dry periods. It is a strong grower and may be taken up and divided in early spring. Be warned, though, that it sulks after being disturbed and may give browned or distorted foliage for the season after moving.

To my regret, the fern doesn't last in water, though I have tried to harden it by soaking. It would make beautiful indoor decoration if a way could be found to keep the fronds from drooping when cut.

Athyrium goeringianum pictum is a mannerly fern, spreading neither by spores nor by running roots as do the villainous hay-scented and sensitive ferns, but merely increasing in girth and in the spread of its painted fronds.

CAMPANULA CARPATICA is far too coarse and sprawly for the small garden. It is neat enough when it first flowers in July but its stems lengthen with the season until they fall away from the center, revealing an ugly expanse of bare shanks. Gardeners tolerate its slovenly habit for the sake of midsummer bloom, but the same long flowering period may be found in more compact forms. *Campanula carpatica nana* and *nana alba* are tidy dwarfs, and the white 'Little Gem' is even smaller and more desirable.

CORYDALIS LUTEA is as much valued for its cool-looking, pale green ferny foliage as for the curious light yellow tubular flowers it bears during most of the summer. The finely cut leaves resemble those of its cousin dicentras but are even more succulent and tenuous-looking. Their substance is as juicy as sea lettuce—even the petioles are translucent—and the whole plant gives so watery an impression that it might be expected to collapse on the first warm day. Instead it stays fresh and crisp all summer, even flourishing in full sun if the soil is well stocked with humus.

CYTISUS KEWENSIS, the hybrid Kew broom, is a semiprostrate shrub as much as three feet in length yet so fine-textured that it can become the focal point of a small rock garden. While the plant will accommodate itself to the contours of an irregular slope, it is most effective when it can launch its cascade of creamy bloom from the top of a cliff or promontory. The main branches hug the face of a rock, not drooping like a willow but springing outward from the tips in a sprightly manner. In early May the short twigs are covered with a froth of pealike blossoms in a delectable shade of primrose yellow, soft yet luminous, commanding attention from the farthest corner of the garden. The olive green stems, virtually leafless, retain their color in winter so that the plant is never without interest.

The flowers of *Cytisus kewensis* have a disagreeable odor of musty clover spiked with creosote. This is noticeable outdoors only if you lean closely over the plant but is very offensive in a warm room—a very good thing for the shrub, as its pendent stems would otherwise be irresistible for flower arrangements.

The Kew broom is hardy to 0° and perhaps as low as —10°. It presents no cultural problems if given full sun and gritty lime soil with a fair amount of humus. Perfect drainage is assured by the raised position it needs to display its waterfall of trailing stems.

DAPHNE GENKWA follows immediately behind *Cytisus kewensis* and should be planted accordingly: the two make a blissful marriage. The daphne is a reticent little shrub, more erect than the broom but with slender branches arching to the ground. Its violet-blue flowers, in shape like the floret of a single lilac, are small but thickly massed. Since both plants bloom naked, the radiance of their complementary colors is undiluted.

If grown naturally, *Daphne genkwa* will eventually reach a height of 36″ with an even greater spread. As a companion for *Cytisus kewensis*, its head should be kept low by pruning or pegging down, so that its cloud of blue flowers may trail among the broom's moonbeam yellow spurs.

As an added inducement for planting them together, *Daphne genkwa* likes the same soil and exposure as *Cytisus kewensis*. Though the daphne is said to be hardy only to zero, I can vouch for its being unharmed at −8°.

EPIMEDIUM YOUNGIANUM NIVEUM was described in Chapter 7 as an invaluable subject for the transitional March–April garden. Though its peak of bloom is early, the epimedium shows a scattering of flowers occasionally in summer and fall. More important, its foliage is a decorative asset throughout the growing season, and for this reason *E. y. niveum* deserves a high place on the list of accent plants for summer interest.

ERICA CARNEA 'KING GEORGE' was cited in Chapter 2 as the only shrub that flowers throughout a northern winter. Like *Epimedium youngianum niveum*, it is a superlative plant, one that deserves to be mentioned so often that it can't possibly be overlooked.

The astonishing performance of 'King George' was freshly (and painfully) dramatized by attempts to photograph the plant blooming in the snow. I took a series of pictures in the Brooklyn Botanic Garden on January 19 after a heavy snow and sleet storm. I had to break the crust in order to uncover the plant and thought the obviously disturbed snow looked unnatural. I went again after a more photogenic fall of light, powdery snow. It was 15° and blowing a full gale. My fingers stiffened with cold and so did the camera shutter: the whole reel was so overexposed that the slides were almost blank. Metal and flesh failed in the bitter cold but the incredibly tough erica remained rosy and unconcerned.

GENTIANA ACAULIS is one of the intractable alpines that cannot adjust its schedule to alien conditions. In its native highlands it forms buds under the snow and blooms when the snow recedes in July, its crown in hot sun and its roots bathed by melt water. In the lowlands, instead of flowering on the heels of the snow, G. *acaulis* adheres to its alpine timetable. Long before the buds are ready to open, they are blasted to chaff by the first sultry days of our tropic summers.

While I kept a stock of *Gentiana acaulis* for the sake of its handsome carpet of foliage, I can recommend it as a flowering plant only to those who garden at higher altitudes.

GENTIANA LAGODECHIANA is a reduced-scale facsimile of *Gentiana acaulis*, not so breath-taking but having the merit of enduring lowland—even city—conditions. G. *lagodechiana* is a variety of the upright, cluster-flowered G. *septemfida* and is in all respects a neater plant. Its decumbent stems typically bear a solitary flower at their upturned tip, though mature plants sometimes carry two or more. The flower is a rather slender tube with flaring lips. The outer surface is the incomparably rich, deep blue which is the gentian hallmark; the interior is spotted blue on a white ground.

Gentiana lagodechiana survives adverse conditions but repays the effort to give it a cool but not shaded position, that is, in a deep crevice or to the north of a large buried rock. It should be given acid soil with plenty of humus, made loose and gritty to encourage deep rooting, and plentiful water to help it through the dog days of late summer when it elects to bloom.

HELIANTHEMUMS, though evergreen shrubs with handsome foliage and a long period of summer bloom, miss top rating as accent plants. Their fault is that they drop their petals at noon and don't open fresh flowers until the following morning. I recall that when I took visitors around my garden, helianthemums called for apology oftener than admiration.

My objection is certainly not generally shared, for helianthemums have been extensively hybridized. They are offered in a range of color from pale yellow through gold, orange, and apricot to a rather harsh tomato red, and down the scale from deep rose to silvery pink and white. Flowers come both single and double; the shrubs are varyingly prostrate, erect, or undecided—the last being open and sprawly.

Helianthemums need a well-drained limy soil, quite dry and in full sun. Under these circumstances they will prove hardy and enduring. Winterkill and the sudden and dismaying dieback that wipes out plants in summer are the result of damp and uncongenial soil.

Since they are fast growers, with stems that tend to lengthen rather than branch, helianthemums should be cut back severely after flowering and again in early spring if they show a tendency to straggle.

IRISES, except for the bulbous sorts that go underground soon after flowering, are an eyesore in the select garden. Their foliage is frowzy, withering at the tip and getting progressively browner as the summer advances. If the dead

parts are cut off, the resulting scarred stubs are just as unsightly. Worst of all, dwarf bearded irises require constant
maintenance of the most tedious and exasperating sort. Their
habit is so open that bare earth is exposed between their bun-
iony rhizomes, an inevitable haven for weed seeds. Since the
rhizomes lie on the surface, cultivating with a tool is impossible. Weeds have to be scratched out with the fingernails; and
if a thick-rooted pest like dandelion or grape hyacinth takes
possession, the iris must be lifted in order to dig the weed.

Even if dwarf bearded irises had flowers made of sapphires
and spun gold, their duration is too brief to outweigh the
plants' demerits. The chief parents of our garden hybrids, *II.
chamaeiris* and *pumila*, are somber in color and carry their
falls so closely curled under the flower that they look as if they
had hiked up their skirts to go wading. Huddled form and
muted color, often with beards of gray-white, smoky amber,
or dull plum purple, predominate in their hybrids. I would
except 'Blue Frost' as a companion for *Tulipa batalinii*, and
'Keepsake,' which owes its clear, bright yellow color and its
orange beard to blood of *I. arenaria*. As for the rest, they can
have a place at the front of the perennial border where their
unkempt appearance will be overshadowed by larger plants.

The small crested iris, our native *I. cristata* and the Japanese
I. gracilipes are charming in every way but as they like some
shade and leafmold soil, they belong in the woodland garden
and not in the rockery.

JASMINUM PARKERI is a Himalayan shrublet of
great refinement. Though not quite hardy enough to endure
in the North, it is so close to the borderline that I have no
hesitation in recommending it for slightly milder climates. My
plant persisted for about six years, losing just the tips of its
shoots in average winters but being cut back drastically in exceptionally cold seasons. Weakened by root disturbance in the

move to Tenafly, it was finished off by the bitter winter of 1962–63.

As it grew with me under marginal conditions, *Jasminum parkeri* formed a compact mound of nearly prostrate stems, short, slender, a lively bright green in color, and set with tiny leaves of the same fresh hue. Since it was unavoidably pruned by winter damage, I can't say how broadly its mat might spread in a warmer region. It never flowered for me but Carl Starker says that it carries large yellow flowers in midsummer. Even without bloom, *Jasminum parkeri* is a delightful ornament, one to be enjoyed by everyone who can give it a climate only slightly milder than that of the New York area.

POTENTILLA NEVADENSIS, named for its home in the Sierra Nevada of southern Spain, is a quiet plant, not spectacular even when bearing its yellow buttercup flowers. A clump former, not a creeper, *P. nevadensis* has the curious property of seeming to be covered with hoarfrost: the leaves have a silvery sheen and their margins are beaded with glistening drops. I haven't been able to decide whether this is a trick of light reflecting from minute hairs, or whether the potentilla has the faculty of retaining dewdrops. However it is done, the illusion of frost is agreeably cooling on a midsummer day.

POTENTILLA TONGUEI (syn. *P. tormentillo-formosa*) is a plant of such peculiar habit that it needs a carefully plotted setting. Its dark green strawberry leaves form a bold clump 4″ to 6″ high. From their base proceed naked, trailing stems a foot or more in length, bearing a shower of single blooms of a soft apricot color, each petal marked with a rich crimson blaze at its base. The flowers are enchanting but their long stringy stems are totally out of keeping with the massive foliage. If placed at the top of a rock so that the stems fall over its bare face, their skimpiness is accentuated.

The trick in placing *Potentilla tonguei* is to divorce its two elements by letting the flowering stems trail over a carpeting plant such as *Aubrieta deltoidea* or *Arabis sturii*. With a little coaxing, the thin stems can be merged with the mat. The flowers then relate harmoniously with the small leaves of the creeper while the potentilla stands apart as a handsome foliage plant.

PRIMULAS are endearing plants, disarming in their simplicity and unaffected country charm. Many of the familiar sorts—*Primula denticulata* and the *auricula* and *japonica* hybrids—are too large for rock gardens but the hybrids of *P. juliae* are in perfect miniature scale. The best known is 'Wanda,' a dazzling flower that stands on the quivering threshold between crimson and purple, with a deep yellow eye to make it even more brilliant. This is an uninhibited color that must be used with discretion. It looks well with white or pale yellow primroses, surrounded by bluets, or in front of the pacifying *Epimedium youngianum niveum*.

Among the slightly larger primroses, my favorites are the polyantha hybrids that stay closest to their English parent, *Primula vulgaris*, so nostalgically captured in Staffordshire flower pieces. Their light green leaves are refreshingly crisp, while the flowers are of the luminous pale yellow that is the garden's best harmonizer.

Primroses want moist, cool conditions, by choice the bank of a stream; failing that, in soil well charged with humus and perhaps among deciduous shrubs that will give the plants a little broken shade in summer. Primroses are favored by slugs so a supply of poison bait should be maintained and renewed without lapse.

PULSATILLA VULGARIS (syn. *Anemone pulsatilla*) is advanced with reservations. It is one of the first herbaceous perennials to make a show of any consequence. Children are attracted by its buds, wrapped to the ears in shaggy fur coats, an appropriate dress for the cold season. At blooming time, the silky leaves and dull purple, gold hearted cups are pleasing and compact, but later the plant grows rather coarse and ragged. It produces enormous clematislike pinwheels of hairy seeds that float all over the garden, though unwanted seedlings are easily eliminated. As I say, I hesitate to recommend *Pulsatilla vulgaris* for a small garden unless a place can be found where its rampant summer growth will not be out of scale.

RHODODENDRONS are splendid rock garden subjects —not of course the leather-leafed giants but the dwarf and semiprostrate varieties. The Chinese species such as *RR. impeditum* and *racemosum* are rather difficult to keep: they burn in our hot summers and are sometimes killed back in snowless winters.

Far easier, and my favorite types, are the low-growing *R. indicum* (syn. *macrantha*) varieties from Japan, usually referred to as azaleas. Their chief value is their late flowering, from the end of May sometimes until July. All want acid soil rich in humus, and an annual dressing of coarsely screened leafmold to keep their surface roots shaded and fed. While they prefer light shade, they will stand sun if watered in dry spells.

The hazard in growing these azaleas is that they are fatally attractive to rabbits. Since they grow less than a foot high, their tender twigs and flower buds are at convenient dining height. If left unprotected, the tops of the shrubs will be shorn as ruthlessly as if a lawnmower had run over them, and their flowering lost for the year. Since an arsenic-Wiltpruf spray discolors the foliage and may still be evident at blooming time, the only sure protection is to cage the azaleas in chicken wire during the winter when rabbits are most rapacious.

RHODODENDRON BALSAMINAEFLORUM is a strong-growing plant, a springy mat of slender twigs, small leaves, and relatively enormous double flowers. The buds are especially beautiful, retaining a high conical center while the outer petals slowly unfold. Both in form and in its bright coral color, a bud of R. *balsaminaeflorum* might be twin to the Floribunda rose 'Spartan.' The azalea's flowers soften to coral rose as they reach their full size, and are so profuse that the green of the foliage is almost hidden. Because of its flat top, R. *balsaminaeflorum* looks best cascading down a slope where its entire surface can be seen from a distance and not just when the observer stands over the plant.

RHODODENDRONS 'GUMPO' and 'PINK GUMPO' are entrancing shrubs, almost completely prostrate and bearing extravagantly large frilled flowers. The white form of 'Gumpo' has always been a shy flowerer with me, but the one known in the trade as 'Pink Gumpo' is a jewel. In mid-June its bright green cushion is covered with pale pink, white-centered flowers, not tubular like most azaleas but as flat and ruffled as a fancy petunia. The effect is feminine and delicate yet the flowers are so lavishly produced that their combined impact is quite imposing. If the rock garden has room for only one azalea, 'Pink Gumpo' would be first choice. Let me stress again the importance of protecting these low azaleas against the ravages of rabbits if you hope to have a display of flowers and not of severed twigs.

TOWNSENDIA EXSCAPA is another Western American alpine, this time not from the snow-watered Canadian Rockies but from their drier ranges in Wyoming and Colorado. It is a strange-looking plant with thready gray leaves in a tight bunch only an inch or so high, an economical construction that presents little surface for loss of water. It will stand anything our summer can hand out in the way of heat and drought, and asks only gritty lime soil and a heavy mulch of stone chips to keep its crown dry in winter. Compared to the plant's small tuffet, its flowers are huge: fat lilac-pink daisies with mulberry backs, entirely stemless and pressed tightly into the clump. If you have a stretch of scree—a barren mixture of sand, gravel, and broken stone—it could have no finer ornament than *Townsendia exscapa*.

VERBENA CANADENSIS is neither rare nor difficult, nor is it in fact a Canadian at all but a native of our central and southern states. It is an open and sprawling plant with flowers of a rather aggressive shade between mallow and phlox purple—in fact the verbena has little to recommend it except a flowering season from May to killing frost. Since this enlivens the rock garden in its drab period, it is worth a little effort to minimize the verbena's bad features. If set low in a channel between rocks, its 8″ height is diminished and its spread compressed. To keep the patch from being static, let it flow down a diagonal ravine and then gather again behind a rock on a lower level.

Verbena canadensis has handsome leaves, deeply toothed and crinkled, but the plant is too lax to make a compact clump. Since it seeds freely, seedlings can be used to reinforce the planting to make it as dense as possible.

Verbena canadensis is said to vary from white and pink to near-blue. I have never seen any but the familiar rose-purple but the more amenable colors would be worth searching for. In its common form the verbena had best be kept to itself or associated with white flowers such as the dwarf varieties of *Campanula carpatica*.

The plants I have discussed are not found on roadside stands nor in baskets at the supermarket. They must be ordered by mail from a nursery that specializes in rock plants or —if you are lucky—from a dedicated plantsman in your locality.

I know of no one source for all my favorites. Instead I will list growers, both large and small, in many parts of the country. Half the fun of buying plants is picking them out yourself, both those on your list and the irresistible strangers that demand a place in your garden. Plants bought locally escape postal battering and carry with them an invaluable extra: the dependable advice of the man who grew them.

SOURCES

BULBS

Burnett Brothers, Inc.
92 Chambers Street
New York, New York 10007

The Daffodil Mart
Nuttall P.O.
Gloucester Co., Virginia
(Alec Gray's miniatures,
species and hybrids)

P. de Jager & Sons Inc.
188 Asbury Street
South Hamilton
Massachusetts

Delkin's Bulbs
4205 Hunts Point Road
Bellevue, Washington
(hardy cyclamen)

Alexander Irving Heimlich
71 Burlington Street
Woburn, Massachusetts

J. A. Mars
Derreen
Haslemere
Surrey, England
(rare bulbs)

Walter Marx Gardens
Boring, Oregon

Geo. W. Park Seed Co., Inc.
Greenwood, South Carolina

Mary Mattison van Schaik
Cavendish, Vermont

Wallace & Barr Ltd.
The Nurseries
Marden, Kent, England

PLANTS

Alexander's Blueberry
  Nurseries
1234 Wareham Street
Route 4
Middleboro, Massachusetts
(*Phlox nivalis* and *subulata*
hybrids)

Alpenglow Gardens
13328 King George Highway
North Surrey, B.C., Canada

American Perennial Gardens
D-6975 Dover Street
Garden City, Michigan

Barnhaven Gardens
Box 218
Gresham, Oregon
(primroses)

Goodwill Garden
Route 1
Scarborough, Maine
Kathelen Gardens
Durham, New Hampshire

Lamb Nurseries
East 101 Sharp Avenue
Spokane, Washington

MacPherson Gardens
2920 Starr Avenue
Oregon 16, Ohio
(sempervivums)

Mayfair Nurseries
Route 2
Nichols, New York
(ericas, dwarf rhododendrons
and conifers)

Mountain Valley Nursery
Valley Road
Jefferson, New Hampshire

George Schenk
Box 487
Bothell, Washington

Sky-Cleft Gardens
Camp St. Ext.
Barre, Vermont

Stonecrop Nurseries Inc.
Cold Spring
Putnam Co., New York

Thurman's Gardens
Route 2, Box 259
Spokane, Washington

Village Hill Nursery
Williamsburg, Massachusetts

NOTE:

To obtain a permit to import plant material, write to United States Department of Agriculture, Bureau of Entomology and Plant Quarantine, 209 River Street, Hoboken, New Jersey. State names and quantity of plants or bulbs ordered and whether shipment will be by air, express, or parcel post.

BIBLIOGRAPHY

General Reference Works

Bailey, L. H. *The Standard Cyclopedia of Horticulture*. New York: The Macmillan Co., 1914.

Curtis, William. *Curtis's Botanical Magazine*. Now published by the Royal Horticultural Society. 1787—.

The Royal Horticultural Society. *Dictionary of Gardening*. Edited by Fred J. Chittenden, and others. 2d ed. by Patrick M. Synge. 4 vols. Supplement edited by Patrick M. Synge, and others. London: Oxford University Press, 1956.

The Journal of the Royal Horticultural Society. Various issues.

Specialized Works

Bailey, L. H. *The Garden of Bellflowers in North America*. New York: The Macmillan Co., 1953.

Bowles, E. A. *A Handbook of Crocus and Colchicum for Gardeners*. London: The Bodley Head, Ltd. Revised edition 1952.

—— *A Handbook of Narcissus*. London: Martin Hopkinson, Ltd., 1934.

—— *My Garden in Spring*. London: T. C. & E. C. Jack, 1914.

—— *My Garden in Summer*. London: T. C. & E. C. Jack, 1914.

—— *My Garden in Autumn and Winter*. London: T. C. & E. C. Jack, 1915.

Crook, H. Clifford. *Campanulas and Bellflowers in Cultivation*. London: Blandford Press, Ltd., 1959.

Dykes, William Rickatson. *The Genus Iris*. London: Cambridge University Press, 1913.

Genders, Roy. *The Polyanthus*. Newton Centre, Mass.: Charles T. Branford Co., 1964.

Gerard, John. *The Herball or Generall Historie of Plantes*. London: John Norton, 1597.

Gray, Alec. *Miniature Daffodils*. Reprinted from the *Journal of* the Royal Horticultural Society, June 1946. Revised September 1949.

Hall, Sir Daniel A. *The Genus Tulipa*. New York: Charles Scribner's Sons, 1936.

Jenkins, E. H. *The Rock Garden*. New York: Charles Scribner's Sons, 1920.

Lee, Frederic P. *The Azalea Book*. Princeton, N.J.: D. Van Nostrand Co., 1958.

Maw, George. *A Monograph of the Genus Crocus*. London: Dulau & Co., 1886.

Miller, Philip. *The Gardener's and Botanist's Dictionary*. London: Law & Gilbert, 1807.

Parkinson, John. *Paradisi in Sole, Paradisus Terrestris*. 1629.

Pugsley, H. W. *Monograph of Narcissus, subgenus Ajax*. In *Journal of the Royal Horticultural Society*, Vol. 58, p. 17, London, 1933.

Stern, Sir Frederick C. *Snowdrops and Snowflakes*. London: The Royal Horticultural Society, 1956.

Synge, Patrick M. *The Complete Guide to Bulbs*. New York: E. P. Dutton & Co., 1962.

Wilder, Louise Beebe. *Adventures with Hardy Bulbs*. New York: The Macmillan Co., 1936.

Wilkie, David. *Gentians*. New York: Charles Scribner's Sons, 1936.

GLOSSARY

Alpine house: a glasshouse, usually unheated, designed to protect plants from storm damage, excess moisture, and humidity.

Anther: the pollen-bearing tip of a stamen.

Bee guide: on iris falls, a yellow or orange line intended to lead pollinating insects to the stigma and anther.

Blade: the broad outer part of the fall of an iris.

Calyx: the external part of the flower, composed of sepals. These are usually green but may be colored like the petals.

Falls: the outer segments of an iris perianth, usually drooping at the point where the blade joins the haft.

Filament: the basal part of a stamen, a threadlike process supporting the anther.

Haft: the narrowed part of an iris standard or fall, nearest the base.

Microclimate: the climate of a small area which—by reason of elevation, orientation, soil, or other factors—may be markedly warmer or colder than adjacent areas of the same property.

Pedicel: the stalk of an individual flower, whether solitary or part of an inflorescence.

Perianth: the nonsexual parts of a flower, usually showy, consisting of petals or sepals or both.

Perianth tube: a slender tube between perianth segments and ovary, serving as a pedicel.

Petal: one of the inner sections of a perianth, usually colored other than green.

Petiole: the stalk of a leaf.

Pistil: the female organ of a flower, consisting of ovary, style, and stigma.

Scape: a long flower stalk, usually naked, rising directly from the base of the plant.

Segment: one of the divisions of a perianth.

Sepal: a section of the calyx.

Spathe: a bract enclosing a flower or flowers, as the calla and skunk cabbage; the semitransparent membranes that enfold buds of narcissus, iris, and crocus.

Stamen: the male organ of a flower, consisting of anther and filament.

Standards: the erect, inner segments of an iris flower.

Stigma: the upper part of the pistil, usually sticky, which receives the pollen.

Stigmata: the divisions and subdivisions of the stigma.

Style: the middle part of a pistil, connecting ovary and stigma.

Style branches: in an iris flower, the expanded style which carries on its underside the stigma and stamen. The style branch follows the curve of the haft and forms a tunnel over it.

Umbel: an inflorescence with stalked flowers arising from a single point.

Whorl: a ring of organs all in one plane.